"*Epic Vegan Quick and Easy* is a bright, innovative collection brimming with creativity and a wide array of flavor."

—Miyoko Schinner, founder & CEO, Miyoko's Creamery

"Dustin takes *Epic Vegan* to the next level with tons of quick and easy ways to eat more plant-based comfort food."

—Lauren Toyota, creator of Hot for Food and bestselling author of *Vegan Comfort Classics*

"This book is a total feast for the senses, as friendly to use as it is gorgeous. Bravo!"

—Jason Wrobel, celebrity vegan chef, cooking channel TV star & host of *This Might Get Uncomfortable* podcast

"Not only are the recipes in this book simple and easy to make, they are also delicious with bold flavors and enough variety to keep you satisfied and coming back for more."

—Robin Robertson, author of *Vegan Planet*, *The Plant Protein Revolution Cookbook*, *The Plant-Based Slow Cooker*, and many more

"What a lovely book! No junky, ultra-processed ingredients, just truly helpful recipes to add to everyone's everyday repertoire."

—Lagusta Yearwood, author of *Sweet + Salty* and owner of Lagusta's Luscious

"If you want healthy plant-forward cooking on the table in minutes, this book is for you!"

—Eric Adams, former New York State Senator and author of *Healthy at Last*

"Every recipe in this book packs in the yum-factor with minimal ingredients—it takes the intimidation out of vegan cooking and makes it something everyone will enjoy!"

—Devon O'Brien, senior food editor, *EatingWell* magazine

"*Epic Vegan Quick and Easy* will recharge any seasoned vegan chef with its must-make imagery and inspire plant-based newcomers seeking truly doable recipes."

—Chefs Kate Jacoby and Rich Landau, Vedge Restaurant

"Big, hearty, fun one-sheet meals and epic and easy weeknight options: Dustin brings something for cooks of every skill level."

—Terry Hope Romero, author of *Show Up for Salad*, *Salad Samurai*, and *Vegan Eats World*

"*Epic Vegan Quick and Easy* is guaranteed to level-up your cooking game. You won't be able to flip through the pages of this without dropping everything and running to the kitchen to whip up some magic."

—Michelle Cehn, co-author of *The Friendly Vegan Cookbook*

EPIC VEGAN

QUICK-AND-EASY

SIMPLE ONE-POT AND ONE-PAN PLANT-BASED RECIPES

DUSTIN HARDER

FAIR WINDS

Brimming with creative inspiration, how-to projects, and useful information to enrich your everyday life, Quarto Knows is a favorite destination for those pursuing their interests and passions. Visit our site and dig deeper with our books into your area of interest: Quarto Creates, Quarto Cooks, Quarto Homes, Quarto Lives, Quarto Drives, Quarto Explores, Quarto Gifts, or Quarto Kids.

First Published in 2021 by Fair Winds Press, an imprint of The Quarto Group, 100 Cummings Center, Suite 265-D, Beverly, MA 01915, USA.
T (978) 282-9590 F (978) 283-2742
QuartoKnows.com

Fair Winds Press titles are also available at discount for retail, wholesale, promotional, and bulk purchase. For details, contact the Special Sales Manager by email at specialsales@quarto.com or by mail at The Quarto Group, Attn: Special Sales Manager, 100 Cummings Center, Suite 265-D, Beverly, MA 01915, USA.

25 24 23 22 21 1 2 3 4 5

ISBN: 978-1-59233-986-0

Digital edition published in 2021
eISBN: 978-1-63159-974-3

Library of Congress Cataloging-in-Publication Data
Harder, Dustin, author.
Epic vegan quick and easy : simple plant-based one-pot and one-pan recipes / Dustin Harder.
Beverly, MA : Fair Winds Press, 2021. | Includes index.
ISBN 9781592339860 (hardcover) | ISBN 9781631599743 (ebook)
1. Vegan cooking. 2. One-dish meals. 3. Quick and easy cooking. 4. Cookbooks.
LCC TX837 .H3628 2021 (print) | LCC TX837 (ebook) | DDC 641.5/6362--dc23
LCCN 2020038461 (print) | LCCN 2020038462 (ebook)

Design: www.traffic-design.co.uk
Page Layout: www.traffic-design.co.uk
Photography: Ashley Madden from riseshinecook.ca, @riseshinecook (except for pages 12, 27, 74, 150, 156 via Shutterstock and pages 21, 50, 129, 141, 172, 176, 181 by Dustin Harder)

Printed in China

FOR MY MOM, MARILYNN

A TRUE WONDER WOMAN WHO ALWAYS MAKES THE HARDEST THINGS IN LIFE SEEM QUICK AND EASY. THANK YOU FOR FIERCELY NURTURING MY PASSION TO CREATE FROM THE BEGINNING, I'M FOREVER GRATEFUL. THIS BOOK IS FOR YOU. I LOVE YOU.

CONTENTS

WHY EPIC VEGAN QUICK AND EASY?

Your time is important, and there are only so many hours in the day. This book allows you to effortlessly pull together epic flavors into dishes that are fast and fun to make. You'll have nutrient-packed meals ready in no time for you, your family, and your friends.

Creating a wildly delicious meal in minutes has become a passion of mine. When I wrote the original *Epic Vegan* cookbook, the concept was much more involved and had me in the test kitchen for hours making over-the-top recipes. At the end of a long testing day, I would toss the scraps from my test recipes on a sheet pan and roast them for 20 to 30 minutes. Then I would serve them up on a bed of greens for dinner—and also have lunch prepared for the next day!

That's when I realized that the continuation of *Epic Vegan* needed to be a quick and easy version that burst with vibrant, flavorful, and functional recipes.

First and foremost, I'm a musical theater nerd who likes to cook. Translation: I'm a home cook at heart who got tired of the bus and truck (i.e., touring in musicals) and went to culinary school on a whim. The universe handed me a chef's knife and an apron and now I'm a home cook with chef's tendencies.

In the Back to Basics chapter I offer simple and fast ways to prepare meal staples and even super simple tips for using vegetable scraps from recipes in the book to eliminate waste. I've also included a meal prep suggestion section (page 16) that offers recipe pairings to set you up for the week and help you make the most efficient use of this book and your time. In the chapters, you will find recipes loaded with character and flavor—from the Stress-Free Reuben Burger (page 101) and Loaded Sheet-Pan Nachos (page 72) to the Punk Cheddah Mac Bake (page 157) and Mushroom Carnitas and Brussels Burritos with Sweet Red Onion (page 108)—there is something to satisfy even the pickiest of eaters. I've even offered up my Spiced Hot Chocolate S'mores Brownies (page 182), a simplified version of the cake I made when competing on the Food Network. It comes together in minutes and is a crowd-pleaser!

It's worth mentioning that all of the recipes come together quickly. And most are ready to eat right away! A few require a longer baking or cooling time, but don't let this stop you from attacking these recipes. I personally love to make something and walk away from it knowing I have a delicious meal waiting for me when hunger strikes.

This book is not just for vegans. It was written for anyone who likes easy and delicious food. If you are new to veganism or just curious about vegan food, great! This book will offer some easily accessible new options for you to start you on your way. If you are a vegan veteran who was making your own soymilk in 1985, thank you for being a crusader. I know this book will offer some new and exciting twists in your already expansive arsenal. If you are the person who constantly says, "I wish I could cook," I urge you to toss out any concerns about "not being a cook." Tie those apron strings up because this book will hold your hand and give you the confidence you have been craving to get in the kitchen and create!

Fast, fun, and creative, that's the *Epic Vegan Quick and Easy* way. It's time to relax and play with your food. It's time to get *epic*.

THIS BOOK IS NOT JUST FOR VEGANS. IT WAS WRITTEN FOR ANYONE WHO LIKES EASY AND DELICIOUS FOOD.

INGREDIENTS

Two camps of people consume food void of animal or animal by-products: the vegans and the whole-food plant-based crowd. Listen, I support both, and I urge you not to get caught up on labels like this. You do you. Do what feels right to you, stay in your own lane, and let everyone else argue over it. I use a mix of what are considered vegan products and also whole-food plant-based ingredients. Some are vegetable-forward recipes, and others call on store-bought vegan mayonnaise or vegan sausage, etc. I don't feel bad about this and I'm not apologizing for it, and neither should you. It's a balance, and this book offers options for everyone. This is purposeful. Using a variety of easy-to-find ingredients makes these recipes accessible and welcoming no matter where you are on your food journey.

The vegan world of possibilities has expanded rapidly over the last few years. Nutritional yeast is now easily found on supermarket shelves, and supermarkets are creating their own lines of plant-based products. For that reason, I will list just a few ingredients that may be new to you, but that I promise are worth the search at the supermarket. If your local store doesn't have it, ask the manager to stock it! And while you are waiting for it to be stocked, order it online and get cooking.

CHILI GARLIC SAUCE

Chili garlic sauce has become one of my favorite ingredients. A little goes a long way, and it can instantly elevate a dish to the next level. The sauce combines coarsely ground chilies and garlic creating a full-bodied flavor in recipes. It can be found in the international aisle at the supermarket, usually near the sriracha.

FLAX MEAL

Flax meal is used to create a "flax egg," which acts as a leavening agent, just as the egg would, in a baked good. If you can't find flax meal, you can grind up flaxseed in a coffee or spice grinder to make the meal. If you are allergic to flax, use an equal amount of chia seeds ground up into a meal for the same results.

HIMALAYAN BLACK SALT (KALA NAMAK)

This salt is actually pink. It is a kiln-fired rock salt used in South Asia with a sulfurous, pungent-smell making it the perfect spice to add to any "egg" dish. In this book, you will see it is always optional: It won't make or break a recipe. It simply enhances it. Meaning, if you don't have it, "fuggetaboutit" and proceed without. The spice is easy to find at spice markets but, as I do with the nutritional yeast, I order a big bottle online. Buy one bottle online and it will last you a long time. It's totally worth it, promise!

JACKFRUIT

Jackfruit is an exotic fruit native to South India. It is also seasonal. For this reason, I use canned jackfruit in these recipes. The texture of jackfruit is like shredded meat and is somewhat flavorless allowing it to take on the flavor of other ingredients. Canned jackfruit can be found in the supermarket with the canned goods. Frozen jackfruit is available, though it is less common than canned. It is also shelved in the international aisle or sometimes in the cooler with tofu and alternative meats.

MISO

While you may be familiar with miso soup, you may not be familiar with the miso paste, which is the base of the soup. Miso is a paste made from fermented soybeans, and it is very versatile. It's an excellent ingredient to make vegan recipes a home run, offering the umami pop of salty, tangy, and savory flavors. It is often found in the produce section in the cooler with the tofu. There are also shelf stable brands in the international aisle. In a serious Nancy Drew hunt for it you may have to seek out your local Asian market or, again, there is no shame in ordering the shelf stable variety online. In a pinch, I have been able to sub out miso with Dijon mustard when desperate.

NONDAIRY MILK

Some recipes call for either unsweetened soy or almond milk. The recipes were tested with these, and they are the most commonly purchased nondairy milks. However, usually your nondairy milk of choice will work, be it cashew, oat, or macadamia milk. Though I urge you not to substitute with thinner options such as rice milk or milk with strong flavors such as hemp milk. Stick to soy, oat, and nut-based milks, and the recipes will turn out as intended.

NUTRITIONAL YEAST

This comes in a powder or flake form with a nutty and cheesy flavor and is rich in B12 vitamins. It is a great swap for Parmesan cheese and used in many recipes to create the cheesy flavors we love. It has become increasingly easy to find over the last few years, but I actually love to order mine online in bulk to stock up. I go through it fast!

NUTS

When nuts are called for in these recipes, the purest form of the nut is required (unless otherwise specified). Choose nuts that are unsalted and raw (e.g., raw cashews). Save by buying in bulk! If you have a nut allergy, try subbing out with a neutral seed such as sunflower seeds. If you're using cashews for a sauce and you don't have a high-speed blender, be sure to soak cashews overnight or boil them in water for ten minutes and drain before making the recipe.

TAHINI

Tahini is made from toasted ground hulled sesame. It has the appearance of a lighter creamy peanut butter. Tahini is not inherently sweet like nut butters; rather, it has the earthy and nutty flavor of sesame seeds with a little hint of bitterness. It is found in the section of the supermarket with the nut butters.

USING A VARIETY OF EASY-TO-FIND INGREDIENTS MAKES THESE RECIPES ACCESSIBLE AND WELCOMING NO MATTER WHERE YOU ARE ON YOUR FOOD JOURNEY.

TOOLS

This book will call on tools you most likely already have in your kitchen. Standard pots and pans, spatulas, whisks, and a blender. Don't go restocking your kitchen. This book does not require that investment.

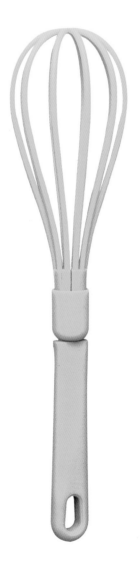

BLENDERS

Oh, the dreaded "do I have to have a high-speed blender?!" question I get at every food festival demonstration I do and class I teach. The answer is "NO!" you do not need to have a high-speed blender to create smooth decadent sauces from nuts, etc. However, there have been such advancements in the world of blenders that it wouldn't hurt to have at least a mid-grade blender. High speed or not, you will be good to go! If you have a high-speed blender, you can skip the nut preparation of soaking or boiling. If you have a standard blender, do the soaking or boiling preparation for nuts. You may want to add just a touch more liquid to get the goods moving around without a high-speed blender, but you'll get there. It just requires a little more patience.

PARCHMENT PAPER AND SILICONE BAKING MATS

Parchment paper and silicone baking mats are used on sheet pans to prevent baked goods from sticking to the pan. In my test kitchen, we use parchment paper mainly because I like to test with what I assume most home cooks will have on hand. The recipes in this book are flexible and allow the use of whichever you are most comfortable with. Wax paper is not like parchment or silicone baking mats. Do not use wax paper for the recipes in this book.

POTS AND PANS

Traditional pots and pans are used throughout the book. If you have ever purchased a complete set (even the cheapest of them), you have what you need for this book. Saucepans, skillets, and stockpots are called on most often. Occasionally I offer the option of a cast-iron skillet. I love cast iron because the heat is distributed much more evenly, creating a balanced cooking experience and less shuffling around of ingredients when cooking. Cast-iron skillets are relatively inexpensive, and they last for years and years. Treat yourself to one if you find you are digging this whole cooking thing. If you don't have one, an oven-safe skillet works in place of a cast-iron one.

SHEET PANS (AKA BAKING SHEETS)

Sheet pans get used a lot in this book. A standard sheet pan or baking sheet is a 11 x 16–inch (28 x 41–cm) rimmed aluminum sheet pan, and I specifically note the measurements if it is important to the outcome of the recipe. For example, the Beyond the Cinnamon Roll Sheet-Pan Pancakes (page 42) require a 11 x 16–inch (28 x 41–cm) sheet pan. Beyond that, it's not that serious! Don't get hooked up on size. Large means a lot of ingredients need to fit on the sheet pan and small means just that, a small amount of ingredients will be used. If you only have a large sheet pan, then that is big enough to handle a recipe that calls for a small sheet pan. You dig?

EPIC YOUR WAY

This book is about creating your epic, your way. Sometimes, when preparing food, we put a lot of pressure on ourselves. This section offers a few tips and tricks to help aid things along with some optional or alternative cooking methods as desired by the home cook. In particular, I want to get crystal clear on gluten, oil, and garnishes to relieve any potential stresses that can sometimes be brought about when reading through a recipe. Take a minute, take a breath, shake off any self-imposed expectations, and allow yourself the freedom to play with your food.

GARNISHES

I can't stress this enough: A garnish is not necessary. I offer options in this book for garnishes because I love them and I have learned how beneficial they are to the aesthetic of the meal. Part of the joy of cooking for friends and family is offering a dish that is just as beautiful as it is delicious. But if you are fast and furiously cooking for yourself on a busy weeknight, use an optional garnish or omit it. Please don't stop yourself from making a recipe just because you don't have the garnish at hand! I do, however, kindly ask you to please always garnish before posting to Instagram. Tag me @theveganroadie so I can see what you are cooking up!

GLUTEN-FREE

I am sensitive to your sensitivities! I honestly think we all have gluten intolerances. Some are affected more than others, and some struggle with celiac. You can sub out any pasta with gluten-free pasta. Use gluten-free tamari instead of soy sauce. For the baking recipes, you can evenly swap in gluten-free all-purpose flour. I try to note the gluten-free option in the ingredient list when possible. Even if you aren't officially "gluten-free," it won't hurt you to try it—and I bet your tummy will be thankful. Not only that, being expansive in trying gluten-free options means you can easily feed that last-minute dinner guest who says, "Oh, I'm gluten-free." You will be prepared!

OIL-FREE

What a fun topic this has become! Here's my two cents: I use oil. I might even say I love oil. I say this without apologies. Oil adds a richness and a depth of flavor and, at times, aids in browning and crisping food to get that desired finishing touch. However, I have enjoyed firsthand the benefits of an oil-free diet in terms of weight maintenance and overall health. Therefore, I support both camps. If using oil is still of interest, but you have a desire to decrease the oil, using a little spray of canola or olive oil goes a long way. I use oil, but feel free to use these suggestions to either eliminate oil or cut back on it.

Oil-Free for Roasting

When roasting ingredients without oil, I use a splash of vegetable broth, vinegar, or lemon juice. Sometimes I even toss the ingredients with a mixture of tahini and lemon juice, then season them with preferred herbs and roast them. Starchy vegetables come out a little drier. You can always steam starchy vegetables first to release the water content and then roast them. Vegetables with a higher water content (e.g., broccoli, cauliflower, cabbage, etc.) tend to dry roast or sauté fantastically without adding oil as the natural water content is released while cooking.

Oil-Free for Sautéing

This is the one that I get asked about the most in cooking classes: sautéing without oil, or dry sautéing as it is sometimes referred to. It's as easy as sautéing vegetables as you traditionally would and adding a couple tablespoons of water or veggie broth as needed, until the desired doneness is reached. It requires paying a little more attention while your vegetables are sautéing so they don't dry out and your pan doesn't burn, but it's easy to master. Vegetables that release a lot of moisture, such as mushrooms, are a great vegetable to practice with when honing your dry sauté skills.

Oil-Free for Soups

When I'm opting to make oil-free soups, I use 2 tablespoons to ¼ cup (28 ml to 60 ml) of vegetable broth in place of the oil. When sautéing, add more as needed, until you achieve the desired doneness.

HOW TO USE THIS BOOK

There is no right or wrong way to use this book. The recipes have been tested over and over by me and a very dedicated and talented group of recipe testers to give you foolproof recipes. Now you can get in the kitchen and cook something up without concern that you are fudging it up or wasting your very precious time.

If you are a visual learner, I find YouTube University to be very helpful. There is always someone who took the time to create a "how-to" video on YouTube, and you should take advantage of it! From dicing an onion to flambéing (no, we will not flambé in this book) there's a video for that—and it's free! You can also find tips and tricks peppered throughout my series *The Vegan Roadie* from myself and other chefs across the globe!

While there isn't a dedicated meal prep chapter, take advantage of the meal prep suggestions on page 16. While testing the recipes, I found myself with a delightful array of meal prep options, and I was thrilled to put together a useful list of them for you.

And hey, while this notion seems basic, before you dive in, read the recipe you want to cook in its entirety before you get started. Make your shopping list before you go to the grocery store, though I think you will find that many ingredients in these recipes are already in your pantry. Enter your kitchen with intention and purpose, and chop, dice, and peel your ingredients before you turn up the heat on the stove! Follow these easy steps and you will be epic AF.

From enjoying snacks on the couch to creating a satiating main course, there is something for everyone—including desserts! So, get out your Post-it notes and tab this book up with your list of "must make" recipes! I leave you with this final nugget of wisdom. In the words of my dear friend and Broadway and television powerhouse J. Elaine Marcos, "learn the rules, and then break them" to get the best results that are authentic to you.

I hope you will use this book and then return to it again and again to create your favorite recipes. Give them your own creative spin as you get comfortable. Dare I say, you will be cooking up *Epic Vegan Quick and Easy* in no time!

LEARN THE RULES AND THEN BREAK THEM TO GET THE BEST RESULTS THAT ARE AUTHENTIC TO YOU.

MEAL PREP SUGGESTIONS

COMBO 1:
Garlicky Nooch Broccoli
and Potatoes (page 126) and
massaged kale (page 27)

COMBO 2:
Lemon Garlic and Thyme, Oh
My! (page 137) and baked tofu
(page 34)

COMBO 3:
Rainbow Vegetables and Tofu
Sheet Pan (page 120), Basic
Betty Beans (page 21), and
sautéed spinach (page 26)

COMBO 4:
Good Goddess Choppy Salad
(page 124) and Say Cheese!...
and Broccoli Soup (page 89)

COMBO 5:
Dustin's Favorite Summer Salad
(page 130) and massaged kale
(page 27)

COMBO 6:
Baked Not So Stir-Fry in a Flash
(page 145) and Cauliflower Rice
for the Win (page 32)

COMBO 7:
Whole Roasted Maple-Dijon
Cauliflower (page 148) and
Quick Quinoa (page 20)

COMBO 8:
Not-So-Tuna Jackfruit Melt
(page 128) and Good Goddess
Choppy Salad (page 124)

COMBO 9:
Bahn Mi Arugula Bowl (page
122) and Easy Black Bean Soup
(page 92)

COMBO 10:
Italian Cheesy Herbed Tofu
and Kale Bowl (page 123) and
5-Ingredient Pasta Fagioli
(page 83)

COMBO 11:
Baked tempeh (page 25),
Rice Realness (page 20),
and sautéed chard (page 26)

COMBO 12:
Basic Betty Beans (page 21),
Cauliflower Rice for the Win
(page 32), and sautéed spinach
(page 26)

COMBO 13:
Maple Balsamic Brussels and Sweet Potato Hash (page 45) and massaged kale (page 27)

COMBO 17:
Easy 5-Alarm 2-Bean Tacos (no tortilla, page 110) and Rice Realness (page 20)

COMBO 21:
Fiesta Quinoa Bowl with Sweet Lime Vinaigrette (page 134) and massaged kale (page 27)

COMBO 14:
Nashville Hot Tots (page 68) and Good Goddess Choppy Salad (page 124)

COMBO 18:
Not-So-Tuna Jackfruit (page 128) on store-bought crackers of choice or cucumber slices

COMBO 22:
Roasted winter vegetables (page 28), baked tofu (page 34), and Rice Realness (page 20)

COMBO 15:
One-Sheet BBQ Mushroom Jack 'n Peaches Sandwiches (no bread, page 105) and massaged kale (page 27)

COMBO 19:
Coco Loco Pad Thai (page 154) and steamed edamame

COMBO 23:
Italian Cheesy Herbed Tofu and Kale Bowl (page 123) and Zippy Zuppa Toscana (page 96)

COMBO 16:
Mushroom Carnitas and Brussels Burrito with Sweet Red Onion (no tortilla, page 108) and Cauliflower Rice for the Win (page 32)

COMBO 20:
Creamy Shiitake and Cauliflower Rice Risotto (page 160) and roasted carrots (page 28)

COMBO 24:
Massaged kale (page 27) and Smoky Tempeh Peanut Satay (page 60)

CHAPTER ONE

BACK TO BASICS: STAPLES TO MAKE THE DULL DELICIOUS

QUICK QUINOA

Quinoa is super versatile and rich in protein, iron, and fiber, making it a great addition to any meal. I love quinoa because it's sort of like a cross between brown rice and oatmeal. It's crunchy, creamy, fluffy, and somewhat nutty all rolled into one. It's the perfect canvas to jazz up any way you choose and then add to bowls or salads throughout the week, making it perfect for meal prep.

+ 1 cup (200 g) red, white, or tricolor quinoa, rinsed thoroughly
+ 2 cups (475 ml) water
+ ¼ teaspoon sea salt (optional)

Combine the quinoa, water, and salt (if using) in a saucepan and cover. Quickly bring to a boil over medium-high heat. Reduce to low heat and simmer for 12 to 14 minutes, until the water has been absorbed and the quinoa has doubled in size. Keep covered and remove from the heat. Let sit for 10 minutes. Remove the lid from the saucepan and fluff with a fork.

Enjoy the quinoa as is or seasoned with your favorite oil and spices. Use ¼ cup (46 g) for a salad topping throughout the week.

YIELD 6 to 8 servings (3 cups [555 g])

TIP

Mix in items you love and make this quinoa a go-to favorite for lunches and meal prep. Try adding in your favorite oils, beans, veggies, spices, crushed nuts, prepared proteins, and even fruits. It's a blank canvas ready to be assigned the flavors you choose—have fun!

RICE REALNESS

Brown rice is preferred to white because it's less processed, leaving more nutrients intact. I chose it as the base here, but use your favorite rice in any dishes that call for rice. Batch cook the rice, double the recipe if needed, and use it for meal prep portions in your weekly meal lineup.

+ 1 cup (190 g) long-grain brown rice
+ 2½ cups (570 ml) water
+ ¼ teaspoon sea salt

Combine the rice, water, and salt in a saucepan. Cover and bring to a boil over medium-high heat. Reduce the heat and simmer for 40 to 45 minutes, until the water is absorbed.

Remove from the heat and let sit, covered, for 10 minutes. Fluff with a fork.

YIELD 4 cups (632 g)

Not all rice cooks the same. Be sure to read the back of the package for specific cooking instructions if stepping out of the brown rice arena. Cutting calories? Gurl, me too! Use the Cauliflower Rice for the Win recipe (page 32) for an immediate calorie slash in place of rice when desired.

BASIC BETTY BEANS

If you are going for quick, you are likely getting canned beans and I support you! Dried or canned, beans are very versatile and add a great protein push. I'm offering a version for dried beans here because let's face it—if you have the time, the dried certainly eliminates the not-so-pleasant aftermath of the canned beans (insert flatulence joke). But you can use either dried or canned as a side dish with a green and protein such as tempeh, tofu, or seitan for a complete protein plate. Or pair with any salad, rice, cauliflower rice, or vegetable grain bowl throughout the week to keep the meal prep game on track.

+ 1 pound (454 g) dried beans
+ 10 cups (2.4 L) water, for traditional soak
+ 6 cups (1.4 L) water, for quick soak
+ More water for cooking

Traditional Soak

Add the beans and water to a stockpot. Cover with a lid and let sit overnight or for at least 8 hours.

Quick Soak

Add the beans and water to a stockpot. Cover with a lid and bring to a boil for 5 minutes. Remove from the heat and let sit covered for 1 hour.

To prepare the beans, drain and rinse them. Return the beans to the pot. Add water again, at least 4 inches (10 cm) above the beans. Cover the beans and bring to a boil. Reduce the heat and simmer for 60 to 90 minutes, or more depending on the bean. The beans should be submerged in water the entire time. Add more water, if needed.

The beans are done when they are swollen and tender. They should not be mushy or bursting open. Test the beans by mashing to the side of the pot with a fork or take one out and do a bite test (i.e., biting it to see if it is done to your liking). When beans reach desired doneness, drain immediately to halt cooking.

Beans will keep in an airtight container for 5 days in the refrigerator.

YIELD 6 cups (about 1 kg)

TIP

Add some flavor to your beans by adding onion, garlic, and bay leaf to the water while cooking them. Store cooked beans that you don't use in the freezer for up to 6 months. Portion them into resealable bags or containers. Remove from the freezer when ready to use. Thaw and use just as you would canned beans.

VEGGIE PASTA-BILITIES

First things first, I'm not claiming vegetables are a direct substitute for pasta. So before you go posting a negative book review on the internet, let me just say pasta is pasta and ain't nothing can replace it! That being said, I do like vegetable "pasta" paired with fresh vegetables, herbs, and sauces. Use a spiralizer, hand vegetable peeler (great spiralizer-free option), mandolin, or even a julienne vegetable peeler to create a batch of vegetable noodles at the beginning of the week. Dive into one of the options below to give some pep to your weekly meal prep!

FOR PESTO AND ZUCCHINI NOODLES:

+ 4 cups (420 g) spiralized or peeled noodle green zucchini, washed with skin on (2 large zucchini)

+ 1 batch presto pesto (page 50)

+ 1 cup (150 g) halved cherry tomatoes

+ Instant Almond Cheese Crumble (page 33, optional)

+ Crushed red pepper (optional)

Add the zucchini noodles and pesto to a bowl and toss until well combined. Portion into 4 prep containers and top with cherry tomatoes. Sprinkle with Instant Almond Cheese Crumble and crushed red pepper (if using). This is best served right away; use it within 3 days.

FOR CARROT ALFREDO BOWL:

+ 4 cups (245 g) spiralized or peeled noodle carrots, skinned (4 large carrots)

+ 2 cups (290 g) roasted (page 28) or steamed broccoli florets, cut very small

+ 1 cup (235 ml) Alfredo sauce (page 150)

+ Instant Almond Cheese Crumble (page 33, optional)

+ Black pepper (optional)

Add the carrot noodles and broccoli with the Alfredo sauce to a bowl. Toss until well combined. Divide into 2 bowls or prep containers. Sprinkle each portion with Instant Almond Cheese Crumble and pepper (if using). This is best served right away; use it within 3 days.

FOR RAW PERFECT PAD THAI:

+ 4 cups (380 g) spiralized and peeled yellow squash, washed with skin on (2 large yellow squashes)

+ 1 red bell pepper, thinly sliced

+ 1 cup (150 g) halved cherry tomatoes

+ 1½ cups (355 ml) Coco Loco peanut sauce (page 154)

+ ½ cup (75 g) thinly sliced cucumber

+ ¼ cup (13 g) canned or fresh bean sprouts (optional)

+ 4 scallions, thinly sliced

+ Crushed peanuts (optional)

Add the yellow squash noodles, bell pepper, cherry tomatoes, and Coco Loco peanut sauce to a bowl and toss to combine. Divide the vegetable mixture between 4 bowls. Fan the cucumber slices along the inside of each bowl on one side between the veggie noodles and the edge of the bowl. Top with bean sprouts, scallions, and crushed peanuts (if using). This is best served right away; use it within 3 days.

YIELD 4 servings

TIP

Spiralizing isn't just for vegetables. One of my absolute favorite snacks is a spiralized apple or pear with the Coco Loco peanut sauce (page 154). Core the apple or pear and spiralize as you would a vegetable and toss with sauce.

TASTY TEMPEH VARIATIONS

Tempeh remains an awesome addition to meal prep. It's high in protein and great for gut health. Its hearty texture provides a satisfying accompaniment to any main dish, salad, or bowl. Some prefer tempeh when steamed first as it can sometimes have a minimal bitter taste. The steaming removes this potential unwanted flavor profile.

STEAMING

+   1 block (8 ounces/225 g) tempeh, cut widthwise into 8 strips

Place a steamer basket in a large pot and add enough water so it comes up to just beneath the steamer basket. Add the tempeh and cover. Bring the water to a boil and reduce to a simmer. Allow the tempeh to steam for 20 minutes. Remove the tempeh and let it cool before handling. Add more water as needed so the pot doesn't burn! Eat plain or use one of these variations.

BASIC MARINADE

+   ½ cup (118 ml) olive oil
+   ½ cup (120 ml) soy sauce or gluten-free tamari
+   2 tablespoons (40 g) maple syrup
+   Juice of 1 lemon
+   ½ teaspoon garlic powder
+   ½ teaspoon onion powder
+   ¼ teaspoon sea salt
+   1 block (8 ounces/225 g) tempeh, cut widthwise into 8 strips

To marinate the tempeh, place the olive oil, soy sauce, maple syrup, lemon juice, garlic powder, onion powder, and salt in a small shallow bowl. Whisk until well combined. Add the tempeh and cover. Place in the refrigerator for 30 minutes, flip the tempeh, and let sit for 30 minutes.

BAKED

Preheat the oven to 400°F (200°C, or gas mark 6). Line a sheet pan with parchment paper.

Place the marinated tempeh on the prepared sheet pan, spoon marinade onto each piece, and bake for 10 minutes. Flip the tempeh and spoon the remaining marinade onto each piece. Bake for 10 minutes, until dry and darker in color.

SAUTÉED OR GRILLED

Heat a medium skillet, stove top cast-iron grill, or grill to high. Remove the tempeh from the marinade and sear each side letting it cook for 2 to 4 minutes on each side, until the desired color or crisp is reached. No need to add extra oil to the skillet.

CRUMBLED

Crumble the tempeh and mix with the Basic Marinade, taco seasoning, BBQ sauce, or other seasonings or sauce of choice. Bake or sauté as directed above.

YIELD 4 servings

TIP

Tempeh bacon crumbles is one of my favorite salad toppings. To make bacon crumbles: Mix 8 ounces (225 g) crumbled tempeh with 1 tablespoon (15 ml) soy sauce, 1 tablespoon (30 ml) olive oil, 2 teaspoons (10 g) ketchup, 1 teaspoon smoked paprika, ½ teaspoon sea salt, and ½ teaspoon black pepper until well combined. Follow the sauté or bake instructions. This will keep in the refrigerator for 5 days in an airtight container.

EVERYDAY GREENS

I like to get my leafy greens in first thing in the morning by adding a handful or two to a smoothie. But if I miss that, or if I'm feeling my nutritional game in a big way, I'll pull greens from my meal prep stash and have some with my lunch or dinner. I love greens with a protein, such as tofu, tempeh, or seitan, paired with Quick Quinoa (page 20), Rice Realness (page 20), or Cauliflower Rice for the Win (page 32). Below are three ways I prep my greens at the beginning of the week that serve me well to get my greens in a cinch! The steaming option is perfect if choosing an oil-free variation. Note: The greens in these variations refer to dark leafy greens, such as spinach, kale, escarole, and chard.

SAUTÉ

+ 1 to 3 teaspoons (13 to 39 ml) olive oil or ½ cup (120 ml) vegetable broth
+ ½ onion, thinly sliced
+ 1 clove garlic, minced
+ 1 bunch or 1 package (5 ounces/140 g) green of choice, destemmed if needed and washed
+ Sea salt (optional)
+ 1 teaspoon lemon juice or apple cider vinegar (optional)

Heat the oil in a medium skillet over medium heat. Add the onion and sauté for 3 minutes, until soft and translucent. Add the garlic and sauté for 1 minute, until fragrant. Add the greens, in batches if needed. Cook until all the greens have wilted. Add salt to taste and vinegar (if using). Toss to combine.

Store in an airtight container for up to 1 week. They can be eaten cold or reheated on stove top or in the microwave.

STEAM

+ 1 bunch or 1 package (5 ounces/140 g) green of choice, destemmed if needed and washed
+ Sea salt (optional)

Place a steamer basket in a large pot and add enough water so it comes up to just beneath the steamer basket. Add salt (if using); it will flavor the greens slightly. Fill the steamer basket with the greens, cover, and bring to a boil. The steam will wilt the greens in 1 to 3 minutes.

Store in an airtight container for up to 1 week. They can be eaten cold or reheated on the stove top or in the microwave.

MASSAGED

+ 1 bunch or 1 package
  (5 ounces/140 g) green
  of choice, destemmed if
  needed and washed

+ 1 to 2 teaspoons olive oil or
  ¼ avocado, pitted and peeled

+ Sea salt

In a bowl, combine the greens and
olive oil or avocado. Using your hands
to massage the greens. Work the fat
of the oil or avocado into the pieces
for 2 to 3 minutes, until the green
has gotten softer and smaller and
the oil or avocado completely covers
all of the pieces. Salt to taste,
if desired.

Store in an airtight container for
3 to 5 days and use as needed.

Avocado massaged greens should
be consumed on the same day.

YIELD 4 servings

TIP

I use massaged kale most often.
It keeps its structure more than
the other variations. It also lends
itself nicely to grain bowls and
salads throughout the week or
when putting bowls together
for meal prep.

ONE-SHEET ROASTED VEGETABLES

Hands down, roasting vegetables for meal prep has been the tastiest and most efficient method for me. While the vegetables roast, I do the rest of my meal prep. By the time they are finished, I have a tray of bountiful delicious vegetables to add to my meal prep loot! Another option for the health conscious is to steam your vegetables, and I say good on you! As that is straightforward, I'm covering just roasted vegetables in this breakdown.

+   1 to 2 tablespoons (15 to 30 ml) olive oil or cooking spray
+   Sea salt and black pepper

CHOOSE ONE OR A VARIETY OF VEGETABLES:

+   Root vegetables (e.g., carrots, turnips, potatoes, beets), peeled and cut into ½-inch (1-cm) cubes
+   Winter squash (e.g., kabocha, butternut, pumpkin, acorn), peeled and cut into ½-inch (1-cm) cubes
+   Cruciferous vegetables (e.g., broccoli, cauliflower, Brussels sprouts), destemmed and cut into bite-size pieces
+   Soft vegetables (e.g., onions, bell peppers, mushrooms, tomatoes, asparagus, summer squash), trimmed and diced

Preheat the oven to 425°F (220°C, or gas mark 7). Line a sheet pan with parchment paper. Transfer vegetables to the prepared sheet pan and toss with olive oil or a light layer of cooking spray. Each vegetable should be coated, but there shouldn't be a pool of oil on the sheet pan. Sprinkle with salt and pepper to taste.

Root vegetables:
Bake for 30 to 40 minutes.

Winter squash:
Bake for 20 to 30 minutes.

Cruciferous vegetables:
Bake for 15 to 20 minutes.

Soft vegetables:
Bake for 15 to 20 minutes.

Flip once halfway through baking and roast, until browned and fork-tender.

MIX AND MATCH

Choose a vegetable from each category and add them to the sheet pan as the baking time increases. For example, add a root vegetable to a prepared sheet pan and bake for 10 minutes. Then add a winter squash and bake for 10 minutes. Flip the root vegetables and winter squash, and add cruciferous and soft vegetables to the mix. Roast for 15 to 20 minutes, flipping the soft and cruciferous vegetables halfway through. Roast until everything is browned and fork-tender.

YIELD 6 servings

TIP

Decrease the oil content by using a light mist of your cooking spray of choice. Play with flavors by tossing the vegetables with an oil you prefer such as coconut oil or avocado oil. To omit the oil completely, follow the oil-free roasting instruction on page 13.

QUICK COUNTRY GRAVY

I value gravy just as much as I do any cheese sauce or easy-to-whip-up dressing. Until now I have always started my gravy base with sautéed onion and garlic. This time around I wanted to keep it quick and easy for you, just like the book says! No veggies to chop, just a simple roux (flour and fat cooked together to thicken sauces), nondairy milk, and some spices. Though easy, this gravy is packed with pricks of flavor from the seasoning! It comes together in a flash when you are waiting for your Effortless Buttered Pan Biscuits (page 44) to bake. It's also delicious on tater tots, french fries, or mashed potatoes.

+ ¼ cup (55 g) vegan butter or (59 ml) olive oil
+ ¼ cup (32 g) all-purpose or gluten-free all-purpose flour
+ 1½ cups (355 ml) plain unsweetened soy or almond milk
+ ½ teaspoon black pepper
+ ½ teaspoon sea salt
+ ¼ teaspoon ground sage
+ ¼ teaspoon garlic powder
+ ¼ teaspoon onion powder
+ Effortless Buttered Pan Biscuits (page 44, optional)

In a medium skillet (cast-iron, if you have one), heat the butter over medium heat until melted. Whisk in the flour for about 3 minutes, until a light golden paste forms. Slowly add the milk and whisk until well combined. Bring to a simmer.

Add pepper, salt, sage, garlic powder, and onion powder, and stir until well combined. Let simmer, stirring occasionally, for 2 to 4 minutes, until slightly thickened and creamy. Serve hot.

This will keep refrigerated in a sealed airtight container for 7 days.

YIELD 1½ cups (355 ml)

TIP

I stray away from calling for freshly ground pepper in my books, mostly because I don't want home cooks freaking out because they don't have a pepper grinder. That being said, if you do have one, this recipe is great for freshly cracked pepper. While ground pepper has a little heat, freshly ground pepper is a little fruity and bright and adds a little more depth to this easy gravy.

CAULIFLOWER RICE FOR THE WIN

Cauliflower rice has become a beloved ingredient, for vegans and nonvegans alike. This beautiful vegetable can be swapped into traditional grain dishes for the same look and feel. Bottom line, it's a super easy way to add more vegetables to our diets. It's a win-win. I have found three ways that I prefer to transform that head of cauliflower into rice, lickity split.

CHOP

Remove the stem and cut the cauliflower into 4 sections on a cutting board. Chop the cauliflower into tiny bits, starting with the head of the florets, and work your way down past the floret. Cut the cauliflower so small it is almost as if you are shaving the cauliflower. Move the rice bits into a bowl before starting each section to create a clean workspace.

FOOD PROCESSOR

Remove the stem and cut the cauliflower into bite-size florets. Process the florets in 3 or 4 batches and pulse each batch until rice forms. Empty each section of processed cauliflower rice to a bowl before starting a new batch.

GRATER

Remove the stem and cut the cauliflower into 4 sections. Pressing the head of the floret to the grater, grate each section of the cauliflower into a bowl creating the rice pieces.

Use this cauliflower rice in place of any recipe calling for grains as you wish!

YIELD 4 cups (about 960 g)

TIP

Portion out the cauliflower rice recipe of choice into 2 to 4 containers to enjoy for a quick meal during a busy week. Cauliflower can become pungent after sitting for several days. It's best to prep cauliflower only when it will be used within 1 to 3 days.

3-MINUTE CASHEW CREAM SAUCE

Cashews are magic. Once I realized how versatile they are for vegan cooking, my pantry hasn't been without a hefty supply. Mind you, we are talking about unsalted, raw cashews with a mild sweet and buttery flavor. They easily take on the flavor of other ingredients, making them ideal for sauces. When avoiding a nut allergy, swap out the cashews for equal parts silken tofu. This may require a little extra seasoning as the base isn't as mild in flavor, but it's a nice swap when needed. Season to taste if swapping out.

+ 1½ cups (205 g) raw cashews, soaked overnight or boiled for 10 minutes in water, drained and rinsed
+ 1¼ cups (295 ml) water
+ ½ teaspoon garlic powder
+ Juice of ½ lemon
+ 1 teaspoon sea salt

Combine the cashews, water, garlic powder, lemon, and salt in a blender. Blend for 1 to 2 minutes, until smooth and creamy. The sauce will keep for 5 days in an airtight container in the refrigerator.

YIELD 2 cups (475 ml)

TIP

This sauce is a versatile base. Try mixing in your favorite herbs and spices if you want to play with your food! Use your favorite fresh ingredients to create your own epic sauces. It also thickens when it sets in the fridge, which makes for a lovely sour cream. Add a little more apple cider vinegar or lemon, as needed to taste, to get desired tanginess for sour cream.

INSTANT ALMOND CHEESE CRUMBLE

This vegan cheese makes any dish pop from tostadas to pasta, and it is super easy to make. If you don't have a food processor, use your blender and pulse it until desired consistency is reached. You will need to scrape the sides down often in a blender to make sure you get all the bits. It will take a little extra time, but you will get to the parmesan-crumble consistency eventually—and it will be well worth it, promise.

+ 1 cup (145 g) blanched almonds
+ Juice of ½ lemon
+ ¼ teaspoon sea salt

Add the almonds, lemon juice, and salt to a food processor. Process until fine and crumbly.

This will keep for 1 month in an airtight container in the refrigerator.

YIELD 1 cup (145 g)

TIP

Reuse a nutritional yeast shaker with a lid (just like a traditional Parmesan cheese shaker). Keep on hand as a staple in the refrigerator to use for soups, salads, and entrees when needed. Blanched almonds are almonds with the dark skins removed. You can buy them blanched already or boil them for 60 seconds and then run under cool water. The skins will be loose and you can pop the almonds out of the skin yourself. I personally loathe blanching almonds and buy them already blanched.

TEMPTING TOFU

Oh tofu, people hate you, people love you. I'd say I have an acquired love for you. When I'm hitting my meal prep strong, tofu provides a low-calorie, high-protein option that also helps me feel very satisfied. I'm not a fan of pressing tofu, only because of time, but sometimes it's necessary, so here are instructions along with a couple basic cooking methods. It's also worth noting my preference is the baking method; it requires less (or zero) oil and cooks evenly on all sides.

PRESSING

+ 1 block (14 ounces/396 g) extra-firm tofu, drained

To press the tofu, tightly wrap the block in dry paper towels. Place the wrapped tofu in a colander and place it in the kitchen sink. Set a small plate on top of the tofu and stack something heavy on top of it (like canned food). Let it sit for 20 minutes to release the water, unwrap, and it's ready for use.

PAN SEARED

+ 1 block (14 ounces/396 g) extra-firm tofu, drained and pressed, cut into ½-inch (1-cm) cubes
+ 2 teaspoons (10 ml) olive oil
+ Sea salt
+ Black pepper

Heat a skillet or cast-iron skillet over high heat for 1 to 2 minutes, until very hot. Lower the heat to medium, add the oil, and tilt the pan to cover the entire surface. Add the tofu, and sprinkle with salt and pepper to taste. This is the most important part: Don't touch the tofu for 4 to 6 minutes. Wait until you start to see a brown color creep up the sides of the tofu. Gently shake the pan. Once all of the tofu moves, flip the pieces with a spatula or tongs. Allow the tofu to sear for 2 to 4 minutes, until nicely browned.

OVEN BAKED, (PRESSING NOT REQUIRED)

+ 1 block (14 ounces/396 g) extra-firm tofu, drained and cut into ½-inch (1-cm) cubes
+ Cooking spray
+ Sea salt
+ Black pepper

Preheat the oven to 425°F (220°C, or gas mark 7). Line a sheet pan with parchment paper.

Spray the prepared sheet pan with cooking spray. Transfer the tofu to the sheet pan and arrange in one layer so the pieces are not touching. Spray the pieces with cooking spray, and sprinkle evenly with salt and pepper to taste. Bake for 15 minutes, then flip and bake for 15 minutes, until browned and crispy.

YIELD 4 servings

TIP

Baked tofu is a great meal prep addition. Multitask to make the most of your time and bake it in the oven as you use the stove top to create grains, greens, and beans for the rest of your meal prep needs!

SCRAPPY VEGGIE BROTH

Chopping vegetables inevitably creates a pile of vegetable scraps. Making vegetable broth with these scraps is efficient, easy, and cost-effective. I also tested this recipe on a myriad of vegetables including red cabbage, which creates a purple broth that works perfectly in a soup with beets! So, don't toss the scraps. Put them in an airtight container and freeze them until you have 4 cups worth to make this fresh broth. You will find little reminders throughout this book that will prompt you to save your scraps for this recipe.

+ 4 cups (weight varies) vegetable scraps

+ 10 peppercorns

+ 4 cloves garlic, smashed, skins on

+ 2 bay leaves

+ Fresh herbs such as rosemary or thyme (optional, see tip)

+ Water

In a stockpot, add the vegetable scraps, peppercorns, garlic, bay leaves, and fresh herbs (if using). Fill the pot with water until it is 2 to 3 inches (5 to 7.5 cm) above the vegetables. Cover and bring to a boil. Reduce to a simmer and cover for 1 hour, until the liquid has developed some color from the scraps.

Set a colander or fine-mesh sieve over a container, large enough to hold and drain the broth. Discard the used vegetable scraps and use as you would store-bought broth.

Broth will keep in the refrigerator in a sealed airtight container for up to 7 days and in the freezer for up to 4 months. To thaw, remove the broth from the freezer and let sit at room temperature. Use immediately as needed.

YIELD 2 to 3 quarts (1.9 to 2.8 L) vegetable broth

TIP

When using fresh herbs, use up to 4 sprigs of fresh herbs per batch of broth. Don't feel limited to thyme and rosemary. Use your favorite aromatic herb you may have on hand (e.g., dill, basil, fennel, oregano, coriander, even mint or lavender) to give this broth a subtle boost.

CHAPTER TWO
BREKKY BITES: PUTTING THE FAST IN BREAKFAST

ALL-IN-ONE BREAKFAST SHEET-PAN BOWLS

Nothing is better to me than a well-seasoned tofu scramble and some crispy breakfast potatoes! Make both at the same time with this one sheet-pan recipe. In thirty-five minutes you'll have breakfast ready for the family without missing Saturday morning cartoons.

+ 4 cups (310 g) frozen hash browns, shredded
+ Cooking spray
+ 1½ teaspoons sea salt, divided
+ ½ teaspoon black pepper
+ ½ teaspoon Old Bay Seasoning
+ 1 block (14 ounces/396 g) extra-firm tofu, drained and crumbled
+ ¼ cup (20 g) nutritional yeast
+ ½ teaspoon ground turmeric
+ ½ teaspoon Himalayan black salt (kala namak) (optional)
+ 1 red bell pepper, roughly chopped
+ ½ red onion, thinly sliced
+ 1 cup (70 g) sliced baby bella or white button mushrooms
+ 2 cups (60 g) spinach, chopped
+ 4 scallions, thinly sliced (optional)

Preheat the oven to 415°F (213°C, or gas mark 7). Line a large sheet pan with parchment paper.

Add the potatoes to the sheet pan and spread in one layer. Spray with cooking spray and sprinkle with 1 teaspoon salt, pepper, and Old Bay. Toss until all the potatoes are coated, place in the oven, and bake for 10 minutes.

Remove the sheet pan from the oven, flip the potatoes, and move over to the left side of the sheet pan. Spray the sheet pan with cooking spray and add the tofu to the right of the potatoes. Sprinkle the tofu with the remaining ½ teaspoon salt, nutritional yeast, turmeric, and black salt (if using). Toss the tofu until the spices are evenly dispersed and push tofu to the center of the pan. Add the vegetables to the right of the scramble and spray everything with cooking spray.

Return to the oven and bake for 10 minutes. Flip everything and bake for 10 minutes, until the tofu has crisped slightly on the top, potatoes have darkened, and vegetables have shrunk slightly in size.

Remove the sheet pan from the oven and immediately sprinkle the spinach over the top of everything. Use a spatula to mix the spinach in until well dispersed, mixing everything together and wilting the spinach as it mixes in.

Divide the mixture among 4 bowls and garnish with scallions (if using). See tip to make the bowl epic.

YIELD 4 servings

TIP

Create your epic with this dish by adding vegan sausage, sliced avocado, a drizzle of sriracha, and a sprinkle of store-bought everything bagel seasoning or Instant Almond Cheese Crumble (page 33).

PUMPKIN CRANBERRY OATMEAL BREAD

Banana bread is amazing. I love it! I have an easy recipe with three variations on my website at veganroadie.com. I also love a nice fall-flare when it comes to a baked good. This bread is perfect for breakfast providing all the harvesty feels with oats, pumpkin, and cranberries. It's the perfect nosh to have lying around if family is hanging out at your house for the holidays. Serve a warm slice with a little vegan butter for a dash of decadence.

+ 2 tablespoons (14 g) flax meal
+ ¼ cup (60 ml) water
+ 1¼ cups (120 g) gluten-free rolled oats
+ 1 cup (125 g) all-purpose or gluten-free all-purpose flour
+ 1 teaspoon pumpkin pie spice
+ ½ teaspoon baking soda
+ ½ teaspoon baking powder
+ ¾ teaspoon sea salt
+ ¾ cup (113 g) dark brown sugar
+ ¾ cup (108 g) canned pumpkin puree
+ ½ cup (120 g) unsweetened applesauce
+ 1 tablespoon (15 ml) vanilla extract
+ ¾ cup (90 g) dried cranberries, roughly chopped

Preheat the oven to 350°F (175°C, or gas mark 4). Line a loaf pan with 3 inches (7.5 cm) of parchment paper hanging over each side.

Combine the flax meal and water in a small bowl and set aside for 5 minutes, until thickened.

In a bowl, combine the oats, flour, pumpkin pie spice, baking soda, baking powder, and salt. Add the flax mixture, brown sugar, pumpkin puree, applesauce, vanilla, and cranberries. Mix until well combined.

Transfer the mixture to the prepared loaf pan, spreading it into the dish evenly until the top is level and flat. Bake for 38 to 40 minutes, until golden brown. Remove from the oven and let cool completely. Lift the loaf from the pan using the overlapping parchment and transfer to a cutting board. Cut into 12 slices.

YIELD *12 slices*

TIP

You can also use fresh cranberries for this! Use ½ to ¾ cup (60 to 90 g) of fresh cranberries in place of the dried cranberries. The end result will have a much tarter pop from the berry, but it will be delicious and the look with the fresh cranberries is very autumnal.

SKILLET BAGEL BREAKFAST SANDWICHES FOR TWO

Beloved breakfast elements on a soft and chewy bagel with toasty crispy outsides—it's a win! Pick breakfast sausage patties that are the size of the bagel you plan to use. Don't be shy to add items you love to this sandwich, such as the Easiest Carrot Bacon Ever (page 57), avocado, or everything seasoning. You can even swap the veggies out in the quick scramble.

+ 2 vegan breakfast sausage patties
+ 1 tablespoon (15 ml) olive oil
+ ¼ cup (30 g) diced onion
+ ½ cup (122 g) extra-firm tofu, drained and crumbled
+ ¼ teaspoon ground turmeric
+ ¼ teaspoon garlic powder
+ ¼ teaspoon Himalayan black salt (kala namak) (optional)
+ ¼ cup (45 g) chopped tomato
+ ½ cup (15 g) baby spinach
+ 2 slices vegan cheese of choice
+ 1 tablespoon (15 ml) water
+ 2 large vegan bagels of choice, toasted (see tip)
+ Sriracha or ketchup (optional)

Prepare the breakfast sausages according to package directions and set aside.

In a medium skillet with a fitted lid, heat the oil over medium-low heat. Add the onion and sauté for 3 minutes, until soft. Add the tofu, turmeric, garlic powder, and black salt (if using). Mix with a spatula, until everything is combined and the tofu has turned light yellow. Cook for 3 minutes, until everything is heated throughout.

Add the tomato and spinach to the skillet. Mix with a spatula until everything is well combined and the spinach has wilted. Move the tofu mixture to one side of the skillet and place sausage patties in the clearing. Divide the tofu mixture on top of each patty. Move the patties with tofu to the center of the skillet and place a slice of cheese on each mound.

Have the lid to the skillet ready in hand and add the tablespoon of water to the skillet. Cover immediately to create steam. Leave covered 40 to 60 seconds, until the cheese melts completely. Uncover and transfer the patty-tofu-cheese covered mounds to each bottom bagel half. Drizzle with sriracha or ketchup (if using). Cover with the top half of the bagel and serve warm.

YIELD 2 sandwiches

TIP

Use butter to go the extra step and get the restaurant-quality touch. Either butter the bagel when it comes out of the toaster, or butter it before you toast it facedown in a hot skillet until browned and crispy. Out of bagels and don't want to run to the store? Use a biscuit from the Effortless Buttered Pan Biscuits recipe (page 44) instead of a bagel.

BEYOND THE CINNAMON ROLL SHEET-PAN PANCAKES

Okay, so here's the deal. While the title of this recipe has Cinnamon Roll in it, here's the bottom line. These are standard delicious and fluffy sheet-pan pancakes that are easy to make and take the stress out of pancake flipping. If you wish to go beyond the traditional pancake (and, dare I say, get *epic*?), I'm offering options for cinnamon roll, triple berry, and even chocolate chip pancakes— the choice is yours! But let's be real, if I just called this Sheet-Pan Pancakes . . . would you have stopped to read the recipe?

FOR PANCAKES:

+ 3 cups (375 g) all-purpose or gluten-free all-purpose flour
+ ½ cup (50 g) organic cane sugar
+ 1 tablespoon (14 g) baking powder
+ ½ teaspoon sea salt
+ ½ teaspoon ground cinnamon
+ 2 cups (475 ml) unsweetened plain soy or almond milk
+ 2 teaspoons (10 ml) vanilla extract
+ Cooking spray

FOR CINNAMON ROLL PANCAKES:

+ 3 tablespoons (42 g) vegan butter, melted
+ ¼ cup (38 g) light brown sugar
+ 1 tablespoon (7 g) ground cinnamon

FOR VERY BERRY PANCAKES:

+ 2 cups (300 g) frozen or fresh mixed berries of choice

FOR CHOCOLATE CHIP PANCAKES:

+ 1 bag (10 ounces/280 g) vegan chocolate chips

FOR CINNAMON ROLL GLAZE:

+ 1 cup (120 g) confectioners' sugar
+ 1 to 2 teaspoons unsweetened plain soy, almond milk, or water

Preheat the oven to 425°F (220°C, or gas mark 7). Line an 11 x 16–inch (28 x 41–cm) sheet pan with parchment paper, enough so it goes up over the edge of the sheet pan.

To make the pancakes:
Add the flour, sugar, baking powder, salt, and cinnamon to a bowl. Whisk until well combined. Add the milk and vanilla, and whisk until just combined with a few lumps. Do not overmix. Spray the prepared sheet pan with cooking spray, pour the pancake batter onto the sheet pan, and spread until it is evenly dispersed.

To make the cinnamon roll pancakes:
Whisk together the butter, brown sugar, and cinnamon in a small bowl until well combined. Drizzle the mixture over the pancakes, then take a butter knife and drag the tip of the knife through the batter from one end of the sheet pan to the other in 3 lines from one side of the tray to the other. Then do the same dragging the butter knife from top to bottom in 4 lines, creating a variation of swirls with the cinnamon mixture in the batter.

To make the very berry pancakes:
Spread the batter on the sheet pan and evenly disperse the berries over the batter.

To make the chocolate chip pancakes:
Add the chocolate chips to the pancake batter *before* pouring the batter on the sheet pan.

For all variations:
Bake for 12 to 14 minutes, or until a toothpick inserted in the middle comes out clean.

To make the cinnamon roll glaze:
Add the confectioners' sugar and milk to a bowl, and whisk until smooth and creamy. Drizzle the glaze over the top after pancakes have cooled briefly for 5 minutes. Drizzle more glaze when plating, if desired.

Cut the pancake in 12 squares. Serve warm with butter and maple syrup, or glaze.

YIELD 12 pancakes

TIP

Make all three variations at once by quartering the batter so you have 4 sections of pancake on the sheet tray. Add one-quarter of the additive ingredients (e.g., chips, berries, cinnamon mixture) as needed for each variation. Leave one quarter of the sheet pan as a plain pancake or have fun and add your favorite pancake fillings to the final quarter. For those with a sweet tooth, the glaze can be used with the very berry and chocolate chip variations as well.

EFFORTLESS BUTTERED PAN BISCUITS

Biscuits make any breakfast special. It's the dinner roll of the morning hour. As I get older, I opt out of the traditional breadbasket at dinner to watch my boyish figure. But I can't stop myself from a fluffy on the inside, crusty on the outside biscuit that billows with a little steam when you crack it open. And these are a win-win from creation to cleanup. Use a baking dish to create the biscuits and omit the use of a biscuit cutter. That way, there's no need to worry about getting sticky biscuit dough everywhere. These go great with the All-in-One Breakfast Sheet-Pan Bowls (page 38) when hosting brunch or a Sunday breakfast with the family. You will also find a Quick Country Gravy (page 31) for biscuit-and-gravy fans. And never underestimate the tastiness of a fresh biscuit served with the Creamy Chickpea Potpie Soup (page 84).

+ 1½ cups (355 ml) plain unsweetened soy or almond milk

+ 2 tablespoons (28 ml) apple cider vinegar

+ 5 tablespoons (69 g) vegan butter

+ 2½ cups (312 g) all-purpose or gluten-free all-purpose flour

+ 1 tablespoon (13 g) organic cane sugar

+ 1 tablespoon (14 g) baking powder

+ 1 teaspoon sea salt

Preheat the oven to 450°F (230°C, or gas mark 8).

To make the biscuits, combine the milk and apple cider vinegar in a small bowl. Whisk together and set aside for 5 minutes to thicken.

Add the butter to an 8 x 8–inch (20 x 20–cm) baking dish. Set in the oven for 2 to 4 minutes, until melted.

Add the flour, sugar, baking powder, and salt to a bowl, and whisk to combine. Add the milk mixture to the flour and mix with a wooden spoon or spatula until it comes together. The dough will be sticky, but do not overmix. Add the dough on top of the melted butter to fill the pan evenly. Use a butter knife to score the biscuit dough. Pierce the dough through with the knife to the bottom of the dish and drag the knife from one side to the other side of the baking dish. Make 3 lines each way to create 9 biscuits.

Bake for 23 to 25 minutes, or until golden brown. Let cool slightly, serve warm.

YIELD 9 biscuits

TIP

Serve these biscuits with raspberry jam for some lip-smacking satisfaction. Might I suggest using these biscuits in place of a bagel in the Skillet Bagel Breakfast Sandwiches for Two recipe (page 41)? Honey, you're welcome.

MAPLE BALSAMIC BRUSSELS AND SWEET POTATO HASH

Back in the days before I went vegan, I tried every diet imaginable. The point-counting system was in that mix. I'll never forget these sweet and tangy Brussels I had once from the point-counting company's recipe bank. I took it a step further here and paired crunchy and savory Brussels with sweet, tasty, and delicately textured sweet potatoes. Mix in spices, oil, and vinegar to bring this perfectly sweet and savory breakfast side dish to life. But hey, add some kale to the mix for a banging lunch that will make your coworkers jealous. Breakfast is really an all-day affair in my eyes anyway.

+ 2 medium sweet potatoes, peeled and cut into ½-inch (1-cm) cubes

+ 2 tablespoons (30 ml) olive oil, divided

+ 3 cups (270 g) Brussels sprouts, trimmed and roughly chopped

+ 1 teaspoon garlic powder

+ ½ teaspoon sea salt

+ ¼ teaspoon black pepper

+ 2 tablespoons (40 g) maple syrup

+ 1 tablespoon (15 ml) balsamic vinegar

+ Fresh thyme (optional)

Preheat the oven to 415°F (213°C, or gas mark 7). Line a large sheet pan with parchment paper.

Add the potatoes to the prepared sheet pan, drizzle with 1 tablespoon (15 ml) of olive oil, and toss to coat all pieces. Bake for 15 minutes. Remove from the oven and add the Brussels. Sprinkle with garlic powder, salt, and pepper. Drizzle with the remaining olive oil and maple syrup. Toss with a spatula to evenly coat the pieces.

Bake for 20 minutes, until pieces of potato and Brussels start to brown and are fork-tender. Remove from the oven, drizzle with balsamic, and toss to coat. Transfer to a serving dish and garnish with thyme (if using).

YIELD 6 to 8 servings

TIP

Another save-the-scraps moment. Freeze the Brussels trimmings and use for Scrappy Veggie Broth (page 35). Even better, save those potato skins as well. Toss the peels in olive oil and salt. Bake at 400°F (200°C, or gas mark 6) for 18 to 22 minutes, until golden and crispy. Transfer to a serving plate and sprinkle with more salt, if desired. Serve with ketchup or your favorite dipping sauce. These crispy potato peels are a hit every time. You'll kick yourself for the years of tossing potato peels in the trash once you have tried them.

BAKED FRENCH TOAST STICKS

As a kid, I always begged to have the frozen French toast sticks in the freezer. I can't recall us having them all too often. Maybe because I gobbled them up so fast! I love this version because I can make ahead and freeze them. They also don't have all the nonsense ingredients store-bought ones have. Baked in the oven, these are crispy, cinnamony, sweet, and savory delicious bites for adults and kids. Served with some premium maple syrup on the side, it's an excellent breakfast for any day of the week.

+ ¼ cup (32 g) flax meal
+ ½ cup (120 ml) water
+ ½ vegan baguette cut into 12 sticks
+ ¼ cup (60 g) unsweetened applesauce
+ 2 tablespoons (14 g) ground cinnamon
+ 3 tablespoons (36 g) organic cane sugar
+ ¼ teaspoon sea salt
+ 1 tablespoon (15 ml) vanilla extract
+ Cooking spray
+ Maple syrup

Preheat the oven to 350°F (175°C, or gas mark 4). Line a sheet pan with parchment paper.

In a bowl, combine the flax meal and water. Set aside to thicken for 5 minutes. While it thickens, cut the bread into 1-inch (2.5-cm)-thick and 4-inch (10-cm)-long pieces, 12 sticks total. A baguette works best.

Add the applesauce, cinnamon, sugar, salt, vanilla, and the flax mixture to a large bowl. Mix until combined.

Spray the sheet pan generously with cooking spray. Dip the bread sticks into the mixture, quickly coating on all sides but not submerging. Avoid making the sticks soggy with the mixture. Transfer to the prepared sheet pan and continue dipping bread sticks until all are coated.

Bake for 15 minutes. Gently slide the spatula under each stick completely and flip each one. Bake for 15 minutes, until dark brown and crispy. Serve warm with maple syrup.

YIELD 2 to 4 servings

TIP

These can also be made ahead and frozen—yup, just like the ones you used to get at the grocery store! After baking, let them cool completely and transfer to an airtight container or resealable plastic bag. Store in the freezer for up to 4 months. To reheat in the microwave, simply arrange on a microwave-safe plate and heat for 30 to 60 seconds, until heated through. To reheat in the oven, arrange on a parchment-lined sheet pan and bake at 350°F (175°C, or gas mark 4) for 12 minutes, or until warmed through.

SWEET AND SAVORY SCONES

Scones are upgraded biscuits full of limitless possibilities. This recipe offers just two options, but I urge you to mix in your own favorite ingredients once you master these two. Some of my other favorites include pumpkin, cranberry, brown sugar, pecan, triple berry, vegan bacon, cheddar, and garlic. Don't be scared. Try your favorite ingredients and play with your food once you get the hang of this recipe! For those who like a little spice, take the optional add-in of jalapeño in the Sausage Cheddar Scones to kick up the heat.

FOR SCONE DOUGH:

+ ½ cup (120 ml) unsweetened plain almond or soymilk, plus more for brushing
+ 1 tablespoon (15 ml) apple cider vinegar
+ 2 cups (250 g) all-purpose or gluten-free all-purpose flour
+ ¼ cup (50 g) organic cane sugar
+ 1 tablespoon (14 g) baking powder
+ ½ teaspoon sea salt
+ 6 tablespoons (84 g) cold vegan butter, cut or spooned into chunks

FOR LEMON RASPBERRY SCONES:

+ 1 cup (150 g) frozen or fresh raspberries
+ 1 tablespoon (15 ml) lemon extract
+ 1 tablespoon (13 g) organic cane sugar (optional)
+ Lemon zest (optional)

FOR SAUSAGE CHEDDAR SCONES:

+ 2 vegan sausages, roughly chopped
+ 1 cup (115 g) vegan cheddar shreds
+ 1 jalapeño, seeded and minced (optional)

Preheat the oven to 350°F (175°C, or gas mark 4). Line a large sheet pan with parchment paper. In a bowl, whisk together the milk and vinegar. Set aside to thicken for 5 minutes.

To make the scones:
Add the flour, sugar, baking powder, and salt to a bowl and whisk until well combined. Add the butter and use a fork, dough cutter, butter knife, or fingers to cut the butter into the flour mixture until the texture has become like sand. Add in the milk and mix with a spatula or wooden spoon until well combined. Do not overmix.

To make the lemon raspberry scones:
Fold in the raspberries, lemon extract, sugar, and zest (if using).

To make the spicy sausage cheddar scones:
Fold in the sausage, cheddar shreds, and jalapeño (if using).

Scoop the batter out in ¼-cup (60-ml) portions onto the prepared sheet pan. Bake for 10 minutes, remove from the oven, and brush the tops with milk. Rotate the sheet pan in the oven and bake for 18 to 20 minutes, until cooked through and the bottoms are golden brown.

YIELD 12 scones

TIP

Use a food processor to quickly cut the butter into the flour mixture. Add the flour, sugar, baking powder, salt, and butter to a food processor. Pulse until a sand consistency is reached. Transfer the mixture to a bowl and follow the directions as written.

PRESTO PESTO AVOCADO TOAST

Avocado toast is where it's at, am I right? Avocado and toast is fine, truly. You can smash an avocado up on dry toast and it will be delightful. But why not take a few minutes and spruce up that dried toast! With just a few simple ingredients your toast goes from "yass" to "ohhhh YASSSSS" in minutes. Skip the pesto if you want and use a drizzle of truffle oil, freshly cracked pepper, and edible flowers for a colorful bite for brunch. See the tip for a bonus avocado toast that is my all-time favorite!

FOR PESTO:

+ 1 cup (40 g) packed fresh basil leaves
+ ½ cup (60 g) walnuts
+ ⅓ cup (79 ml) olive oil or vegetable broth for oil-free
+ 2 tablespoons (28 ml) water
+ 1 clove garlic
+ 2 tablespoons (10 g) nutritional yeast
+ 1 tablespoon (16 g) white miso
+ Juice of ½ lemon
+ ½ teaspoon sea salt

FOR AVOCADO TOAST:

+ 1 avocado, peeled and diced
+ Juice of ½ lemon
+ Sea salt (optional)
+ Black pepper (optional)
+ 2 pieces vegan bread, toasted
+ Crushed red pepper

To make the pesto:
Add all the ingredients to a blender. Blend until there are still some specks of basil visible. Some people like the specks; others like smooth and creamy. Go whichever route you prefer, blending a little longer to make it smooth and creamy, if you desire.

To make the avocado toast:
Add the avocado and lemon juice to a bowl. Mash with a fork just until well combined. There should still be chunks of avocado. Season with salt and pepper to taste (if using).

Divide the avocado mixture atop the two pieces of toast, spreading it out evenly on each piece. Drizzle each piece of toast with the desired amount of pesto, and sprinkle with crushed red pepper. Serve immediately.

YIELD 2 servings

TIP

My all-time favorite quick fix with avocado toast is the lemon avocado mixture at left, topped with a generous drizzle of sriracha and a hefty sprinkling of everything bagel seasoning. I'm not sure you will ever eat it any other way after you try this! But I encourage you to try both ways mentioned on this page and pick your favorite.

MATCHA BLUEBERRY GRANOLA

Much ado about matcha these days! The Matcha Mint Pops recipe in my first *Epic Vegan* book was such a hit, I couldn't resist pairing matcha here with sweet blueberries and crunchy granola for the perfect bowl of yumminess to put some spark in your morning routine.

+ ½ cup (130 g) creamy sunflower or peanut butter
+ ½ cup (160 g) maple syrup
+ ¼ cup (59 ml) refined or unrefined coconut oil, melted
+ 2 tablespoons (14 g) flax meal
+ ½ teaspoon sea salt
+ 1 teaspoon ground cinnamon
+ 1½ cups (144 g) gluten-free rolled oats
+ 1 cup (137 g) raw cashews, roughly chopped
+ 2 teaspoons (4 g) matcha powder
+ Cooking spray
+ 1 cup (120 g) dried blueberries or cranberries

Preheat the oven to 415°F (213°C, or gas mark 7). Line a large sheet pan with parchment paper.

Add the peanut butter, maple syrup, and coconut oil to a large bowl. Mix until well combined. Add the flax meal, salt, and cinnamon to the mixture. Stir until well incorporated. Add the oats, cashews, and matcha. Mix until everything is coated; it will be very sticky.

Spray the prepared sheet pan with cooking spray, transfer the mixture to the sheet pan, and spread in one layer.

Bake for 12 minutes, remove from the oven, and mix. Return to the oven and bake for 10 to 12 minutes, until the edges start to brown. Remove from the oven and let sit for 1 hour to cool completely. It's important to let the granola cool so it sets and sticks together to form some delicious granola clusters. The end result will be a mix of loose granola and some clusters.

Once the granola has completely cooled, add the blueberries and stir until well combined. Enjoy immediately or store in an airtight container for up to 2 weeks. Make it ahead and freeze for several months. It's perfect right out of the freezer as well for smoothie bowls and vegan yogurt.

YIELD 8 to 10 servings

TIP

If matcha isn't your thing but blueberries are, you can still enjoy this granola! Simply leave out the matcha for a super tasty blueberry granola. Likewise, this can easily be made oil-free—just omit the oil! The oil aids in carrying flavor throughout the recipe and coconut adds a lush and decadent texture, but it's not necessary. It will still be delicious without.

THE LITTLE SISTERS CHEESY POTATOES

My mom has two sisters, my Aunt Sam and my Aunt Char. I ADORE THEM. These three sisters (aka The Little Sisters) rotated holidays (Thanksgiving, Christmas Eve, and Christmas Day) throughout my childhood and into my young adult life. This easy to toss together, but oh so decadent, ooey gooey, cheesy, creamy, delicious dish always made its way to the table. All three sisters made it: My mom used cubed hash browns, and my Aunt Sam used shredded. Pick whichever one you like best. These sisters are the hostesess with the mostesess. I miss those Christmas gatherings, but I can always make these to remind myself home is where the heart is, and now you can too!

+ Cooking spray
+ 1 pound (454 g) frozen hash browns, shredded or cubed
+ 1 cup (70 g) roughly chopped white button or cremini mushrooms
+ ¼ cup (30 g) diced onion
+ 1 bag (8 ounces/225 g) vegan cheddar shreds
+ 1 cup (228 g) vegan sour cream or 3-Minute Cashew Cream Sauce (page 33)
+ ¼ cup (55 g) vegan butter, melted
+ 1 teaspoon sea salt
+ ½ teaspoon black pepper
+ 1 cup (112 g) crushed potato chips (optional)
+ Chopped fresh parsley or chives (optional)

Preheat the oven to 375°F (190°C, or gas mark 5). Lightly grease an 8 x 8–inch (20 x 20–cm) baking dish.

In a bowl, combine the hash browns, mushrooms, onion, cheddar shreds, sour cream, butter, salt, and pepper. Cover the top with crumbled potato chips (if using), and bake for 40 to 45 minutes, until the top has started to brown.

Remove from the oven, and sprinkle with parsley or chives (if using).

YIELD 9 servings

TIP

This is a fun one to play with in terms of toppings. You can try vegan BBQ chips or even Fritos… this is not health food! Grab your favorite vegan crunchy snack and crumble it up to bake on top. Then present it as your own creation for any brunch sort of gathering.

PEANUT BUTTER CHERRY CHIP GRANOLA

Crunchy, salty, sweet, and savory all in one. Who doesn't like granola? I'm combining some of my favorite ingredients here for a satiating and flavorful snack I love to have on hand during road trips.

+ ½ cup (130 g) creamy peanut butter
+ ½ cup (160 g) maple syrup
+ ¼ cup (59 ml) refined or unrefined coconut oil, melted
+ 2 tablespoons (14 g) flax meal
+ ½ teaspoon sea salt
+ 1 teaspoon ground cinnamon
+ 1½ cups (144 g) gluten-free rolled oats
+ ½ cup (55 g) pecans, roughly chopped
+ ½ cup (70 g) raw pepitas
+ Cooking spray
+ ½ cup (87 g) mini vegan chocolate chips
+ ½ cup (57 g) dried cherries, roughly chopped

Preheat the oven to 415°F (213°C, or gas mark 7). Line a large sheet pan with parchment paper.

Add the peanut butter, maple syrup, and coconut oil to a large bowl. Mix until combined. Add the flax meal, salt, and cinnamon to the mixture, and stir until well incorporated. Add the oats, pecans, and pepitas. Mix until everything is coated; it will be very sticky.

Spray the prepared sheet pan with cooking spray. Transfer the mixture to the sheet pan and spread in one layer.

Bake for 12 minutes and then flip the granola. Spread back to one layer and bake for 10 to 12 minutes, until the edges start to brown. Remove from the oven and let sit for 1 hour to cool completely. It's important to let the granola cool so it sets and sticks together to form some delicious granola clusters. The end result will be a mix of loose granola and some clusters. Once the granola has cooled, add the chocolate chips and cherries. Stir to combine. Be sure it's completely cooled so the chips don't melt.

Enjoy immediately or store in an airtight container for up to 2 weeks. Make it ahead and freeze for several months. It's perfect right out of the freezer as well for smoothie bowls and vegan yogurt.

YIELD 8 to 10 servings

TIP

Dried cranberries are an easy swap out for this recipe if you prefer them to cherries. Simply use ½ cup (60 g) dried cranberries in place of cherries. The oil helps carry flavor throughout the recipe, and coconut adds a lush and decadent texture, but it's not necessary. Make this oil-free by simply omitting the oil.

CHEAP 'N CHEESY JALAPEÑO GRITS

The combo of melted cheese and spicy jalapeños is always a win for people who like spice. You can't see me, but I'm raising my hand. I'm always looking for ways to house the perfect pair, and creamy grits are the best vehicle for these two. This is easy to make in one pot and a great addition to any brunch spread.

+ 2 tablespoons (28 g) vegan butter or canola oil

+ 2 jalapeños, seeded and diced (see tip)

+ 2 cloves garlic, minced

+ 2 cups (475 ml) plain unsweetened soy or almond milk

+ 2 cups (475 ml) water

+ 1 teaspoon sea salt, plus more to taste

+ 1 cup (140 g) uncooked yellow grits, polenta, or yellow stone-ground cornmeal

+ 1 cup (80 g) nutritional yeast

+ 1 cup (115 g) vegan cheddar shreds, plus more for garnish

+ Fresh sliced jalapeños or pickled jalapeños from a jar (optional)

+ Black pepper

Add the butter to a medium saucepan and melt over medium-low heat. Add the jalapeños and sauté for 2 to 4 minutes, until soft. Add the garlic and sauté for 1 minute, until fragrant.

Slowly add the milk, water, and salt to the pot. Raise the heat to high and bring to a boil. Lower the heat to a simmer, and add the grits and nutritional yeast. Whisk vigorously for 4 to 6 minutes working the lumps out, until thick and creamy. Add the cheese to the grits and mix with a spoon until well combined.

Season with salt and pepper to taste. Serve warm, sprinkled with shredded vegan cheddar and jalapeños (if using).

YIELD 6 servings

TIP

When chopping a jalapeño, wear gloves if you have them. If you don't, a plastic baggie over your hand that handles the pepper will do the trick depending on the size of your hand. Some form of protection is always helpful. Handling a jalapeño and taking your contact lenses out later do not mix. Clearly, I know this from an experience a friend had, not myself. Anyway, cut the top off the pepper and slice the pepper in half lengthwise. Use a small spoon or gently use the blade of the knife to scrape the membrane and seeds from the jalapeño's flesh. Dice as needed.

EASIEST CARROT BACON EVER

I never missed bacon when I went vegan, but I can appreciate that there is a crowd out there that does. I came up with this bacon when shooting the cover photo for the *Epic Vegan* cookbook. I wanted to create bacon that looked just like traditional bacon with the curly sides and carrots did the trick! Shockingly it was super easy to make and had a great crispy crunch and flavor to them. So I wanted to include it in this book for your enjoyment.

+ 1 large carrot
+ ¼ teaspoon smoked paprika
+ ¼ teaspoon sea salt
+ ¼ teaspoon black pepper
+ 1 tablespoon (15 ml) olive oil, plus more as needed

Use a potato peeler and peel long noodle-like slices from the carrot. You should be able to get anywhere from 14 to 20 slices from one carrot. Peel the carrot from top to bottom for the best results.

Place the smoked paprika, salt, and pepper in a small bowl. Mix until well combined.

Heat the oil in a medium skillet over medium heat until hot. Add 4 slices of carrot to the hot skillet and generously sprinkle the seasoning mixture over the top. The slices will begin to shrink. Let cook for 1 to 2 minutes, until the edges start to brown, flipping halfway through.

Transfer to paper towel–lined plate and repeat until all slices have been cooked. Add more oil and seasoning with each batch cooked, as needed.

The carrots should be a light brown color and crispy. Sometimes the edges will even curl like traditional bacon.

YIELD 14 to 20 pieces

TIP

Get the biggest carrot you can possibly find for this recipe because they shrink down considerably during the cooking process. They usually sell single carrots in supermarkets, and they are usually bigger than the ones sold in the bags. Depending on the size of carrot you may run out of seasoning. If the carrot is especially huge, double the spice recipe from the get-go for a continuous flow while you are frying the carrot bacon.

CHAPTER THREE
SNACKS AND APPS: MOVIE NIGHT BITES

SMOKY TEMPEH PEANUT SATAY

This is perfect for parties: a flavorful and vibrant Thai-inspired marinade paired with hearty tempeh skewered and lightly charred. If you are serving it at a party, make a double batch and maybe have more on reserve to toss in the oven as it will become the favorite appetizer of the evening!

+ 4 (6-inch/15-cm) wooden skewers (optional)
+ 1 tablespoon (15 ml) chili garlic sauce
+ Juice of 1 lemon
+ Juice of 1 lime
+ 2 tablespoons (30 ml) toasted sesame oil
+ ¼ cup (60 ml) soy sauce or gluten-free tamari
+ ¼ cup (65 g) creamy peanut butter
+ 2 tablespoons (40 g) maple syrup
+ ½ teaspoon smoked paprika
+ 1 block (8 ounces/225 g) tempeh
+ Crushed peanuts (optional)
+ 2 scallions, thinly sliced (optional)

Preheat the oven to 375°F (190°C, or gas mark 5). Line a sheet pan with parchment paper. Soak the skewers (if using), in a shallow dish of water while preparing the sauce.

Combine the chili garlic sauce, lemon juice, lime juice, sesame oil, soy sauce, peanut butter, maple syrup, and smoked paprika in a bowl.

Cut the tempeh in 3 strips lengthwise and then quarter each strip into 4 triangles for 12 thick triangles in total. The ends will be square, but cut the remaining parts into triangles. Toss the pieces in the bowl until completely coated. Add 3 pieces to each skewer (if using). Transfer the tempeh to the prepared sheet pan.

Use a spoon to drizzle the marinade on each piece. Bake for 10 minutes. Then flip tempeh and use a spoon to drizzle more marinade on the pieces. There should still be about ¼ cup (60 ml) marinade left. Hold on to it. Bake for 10 minutes, until dry. If desired, turn the oven up to broil and broil for 1 to 2 minutes to lightly char the edges.

Transfer the tempeh to a serving dish. Drizzle with remaining marinade, and sprinkle with crushed peanuts and scallions (if using).

YIELD 2 to 4 servings

TIP

I don't steam my tempeh, but many people prefer to steam tempeh before they cook it to release what they call a "bitter" taste. If you do prefer to steam the tempeh, I offer directions to do so in the Tasty Tempeh Variations (page 25).

GAME DAY PUB CHEESE

As a kid, my mom always had this cheese from a company called Schuler's in the refrigerator during the holidays. This is a re-creation of that cheese. The zippy sharpness is addictive. I have taken this to several holiday parties and watched it disappear. One Christmas Eve in Harlem, I watched as the only other vegan at the party pulled up a chair to the hors d'oeuvre table and single-handedly cleared out this dish, cracker after cracker. As usual, I came prepared with backup.

+ 1 cup (137 g) raw cashews, soaked overnight or boiled in water for 10 minutes, drained and rinsed
+ ½ cup (120 ml) vegan lager
+ ¼ cup (60 ml) water
+ 1 tablespoon (15 g) white wine vinegar
+ 2 teaspoons (14 g) maple syrup
+ ¼ cup (35 g) sauerkraut
+ ¼ cup (60 g) tahini
+ 1 tablespoon (16 g) white miso
+ 2 tablespoons (30 g) Dijon mustard
+ 1 teaspoon smoked paprika
+ 1 teaspoon garlic powder
+ ¾ teaspoon ground turmeric
+ ½ teaspoon onion powder
+ ½ teaspoon sea salt

Combine the cashews, lager, water, vinegar, maple syrup, sauerkraut, tahini, miso, Dijon mustard, smoked paprika, garlic powder, turmeric, onion powder, and salt in a blender.

Start the blender speed on low, slowly incorporating the ingredients into the fold. Once the ingredients begin to move, gradually increase the speed. Stop the blender and scrape the sides down as needed to get everything into the mix. Blend until creamy and smooth.

Serve with crackers or vegetables.

YIELD 2 cups (480 g)

TIP

Cashew sauces tend to thicken when they sit in the refrigerator. I'm always impatient, and it's hard for me to wait for this cheese. If you are going to take this to a party, make it 2 days in advance so it thickens slightly and is servable as a spread.

LAYERS OF GREEK DIP

The fresh tangy flavors of Greek cuisine always entice me. What's better than scooping up a bunch of layered flavors with some veggies or chips for a fun appetizer? This is great for parties as it's not the traditional seven-layer dip people are expecting. It's loaded with different textures—from the creamy hummus to the crunchy cucumber—for a very satisfying bite!

+ ½ teaspoon dried dill

+ 1 container (5 ounces/140 g) plain vegan yogurt

+ 1 container (10 ounces/280 g) store-bought hummus

+ ½ cup (64 g) kalamata olives, pitted and roughly chopped

+ ½ cup (100 g) diced cucumber, skin on

+ ½ cup (75 g) grape tomatoes, roughly chopped

+ ½ cup (57 g) vegan block feta or mozzarella or Italian Cheesy Herbed Tofu (page 123), cut into ½-inch (1-cm) cubes

+ Olive oil (optional)

+ Sea salt and black pepper (optional)

+ 3 scallions, thinly sliced

+ Tortilla chips, pita chips, warm pita bread, or sliced vegetables

Add the dill to the yogurt and mix until well combined. You can even add it in the yogurt container if it's a single serve. Spread the hummus on a small platter (5 x 8-inch [13 x 20–cm]), shallow serving dish, or standard-size dinner plate. Top the hummus with the yogurt mixture followed by olives, cucumbers, tomatoes, and feta. Drizzle with olive oil and sprinkle with salt and pepper (if using). Sprinkle with scallions and serve with chips, bread, or vegetables.

YIELD 8 servings

TIP

If using the herbed tofu (page 123) and pressed for time, cool the tofu quickly by transferring it to the freezer from the oven. It should cool completely in 10 to 15 minutes. Remove it straight away so it doesn't freeze and use as needed for this recipe, salads, and bowls.

CHEESY BURGER TATER TOTS

Tater tots are a classic favorite for everyone, with their crisp and crunchy outsides and pillows of warm potato in the middle. I squeal with delight every time a restaurant offers tots as a potato option. Okay, maybe not squeal, but I do get excited. So why not top some tots with nostalgic flavors everyone loves—like the flavors of a cheeseburger! Just pop it on a sheet pan and you have dinner or an appetizer to wow friends and family in thirty minutes.

+ 4 cups (half of a 32-ounce [905-g] bag) frozen tater tots

+ ½ teaspoon Old Bay Seasoning (optional)

+ 1 cup (110 g) frozen vegan ground beef or crumbled vegan sausage

+ ½ cup (80 g) roughly chopped white onion

+ ½ cup (90 g) diced tomato

+ ¼ cup (60 g) sweet pickle relish

+ ¾ cup (88 g) vegan cheddar shreds or Punk Cheddah sauce (page 157)

+ Mustard

+ Ketchup

+ Quick Thousand Island dressing (optional, see tip)

+ 2 scallions, chopped (optional)

Preheat the oven to 425°F (220°C, or gas mark 7). Line a sheet pan with parchment paper.

Spread the tater tots out on the prepared sheet pan and sprinkle with Old Bay Seasoning (if using). Bake for 20 minutes, remove from the oven, and flip the tater tots with a spatula. Position the tater tots close together so they are touching to minimize the toppings falling through to the sheet pan. Top the tater tots with ground beef, onion, tomatoes, relish, and cheese. Bake for 10 to 12 minutes, until the cheese is melted and the tater tots have turned golden brown.

Drizzle tater tots with mustard, ketchup, or dressing, and sprinkle with chopped scallions (if using).

YIELD 8 servings

TIP

Create your epic and turn this into Big Mac Tots with a quick Thousand Island dressing. In a bowl combine ½ cup (115 g) vegan mayonnaise, 2 tablespoons (30 g) sweet pickle relish, 1 tablespoon (15 g) yellow mustard, and 1 tablespoon (15 g) ketchup. Drizzle the dressing over this recipe instead of mustard or ketchup or use it on burgers as desired. Keep refrigerated for up to 2 weeks in an airtight container.

EASILY EPIC CHARCUTERIE BOARD

This is it. The moment to impress your nonvegan friends by creating an epic charcuterie board your guests will swoon over! It's all in the presentation. Don't forget to add a mix of bright fruits and vegetables to complete the look of your board. As always, I encourage you to omit items you don't love and add your favorite items. If vegan meats aren't your thing, just double up the veggies—a charcuterie board is absolutely still in your future! There are suggested measurements below, but ultimately you have to build this according to the size of the board you have. Now go… put the CUTE in CharCUTErie!

+ 2 dips: ½ cup (120 g) store-bought hummus and ½ cup (165 g) jelly or jam
+ 1 cup (128 g) mixed olives
+ 2 vegan cheeses: Game Day Pub Cheese (page 62) and store-bought vegan cheese (block, spread, or wheel)
+ 2 vegan meats: vegan deli slices, vegan pepperoni, prepared and thinly sliced vegan sausage links
+ 3 cups fruit (pick 3, 1 cup of each): blackberries, apple slices, pear slices, grapes, raspberries, cherries, strawberries, or blueberries
+ 2 vegetables: carrots, cucumber, bell peppers, or zucchini, cut into sticks or thinly sliced

+ 1 box raw or vegan crackers
+ ½ cup (55 g) pecan halves
+ ½ cup (68 g) raw or lightly salted cashews
+ ½ cup (57 g) dried cherries or dried fruit of choice
+ Fresh herbs, such as rosemary or thyme

Add the hummus, jam, and olives to small bowls that fit on the board. Place the bowls in a triangle formation on the board with one in the center and the other two at the corners. Add the cheese to the other two corners of the board.

Now comes the fun. Fill in the board with vegan meats, fruits, vegetables, crackers, nuts, and dried fruit. Add serving spoons or cheese knives as needed, and garnish with sprigs of fresh herbs for the finishing touch.

Make this an hour before serving. If you choose apple or pear slices, toss them quickly in lemon or lime juice to avoid oxidizing. Cover with plastic wrap and store in the refrigerator until the first guest arrives.

YIELD 1 epic vegan charcuterie board

TIP

If you don't have a fancy cheese board, simply cover a sheet pan with a fitted piece of parchment for a fun, rustic look! Don't break the bank buying fancy cheese knives. If all you have is a butter knife, work with what you got! I like to use "fancier" jams and jellies for these boards, such as a spiced pear or apricot. If you can't find one, just pour a little juice from a pickled jalapeño jar into some raspberry preserves and BAM, jalapeño raspberry!

NASHVILLE HOT TOTS

"Nashville Hot" has been a craze lately! And I love some spice and tater tots, so I thought no better time to pair these perfect little crunchy pillow puffs of potato with the irresistible Nashville hot spice mixture. While I try to mix ingredients with spices on a sheet pan when I can to eliminate dishes, it is best to mix this recipe in a couple of bowls so the variety of spices get well incorporated into all of the tater tots.

+   4 cups (half of a 32-ounce/907 g bag) frozen tater tots
+   Cooking spray
+   1 teaspoon cayenne pepper
+   2 tablespoons (20 g) light brown sugar
+   2 teaspoons (5 g) paprika
+   1 teaspoon garlic powder
+   1 teaspoon sea salt
+   ½ teaspoon black pepper
+   Good Goddess Dressing (page 124) or store-bought dressing (optional)

Preheat the oven to 450°F (230°C, or gas mark 8). Line a large sheet pan with parchment paper.

Add the tater tots to a bowl and spray with cooking spray. Toss to coat and then spray again covering all tots with a mist of oil. In a small bowl, whisk together the cayenne, brown sugar, paprika, garlic powder, salt, and pepper. Add half of the spice mixture to the bowl of tots and toss to combine. Add the second half of the mixture, and continue to toss tots until all pieces are coated.

Transfer the tots to the prepared sheet pan and bake for 15 minutes. Flip the tots and bake for 10 to 12 minutes, until they are crispy and have darkened in color.

Serve with your favorite vegan dipping sauce. I prefer the ranch dressing from my first book, *The Simply Vegan Cookbook*, or the Good Goddess Dressing (page 124). If you have a favorite store-bought dipping sauce, go with that!

YIELD 6 servings

TIP

This recipe uses about half of a 32-ounce (907 g) bag of frozen tater tots. Use the other half to make the Cheesy Burger Tater Tots (page 64) next time the tot hunger strikes!

QUICK QUESO WITH CHILI-LIME CHIPS

Chain restaurants and queso: Get it together and offer a vegan version already! It's so easy! Never fret, you can now make some for you and your friends lickity-split using one pot on the stove top. Then pick your adventure. Just open the bag of chips and serve alongside the quick queso or add some tangy spice to your store-bought chips with a lil' action in the oven. Adjust the amount of chili powder on the chips to your desired amount of heat.

FOR QUESO:

+ ¼ cup (32 g) all-purpose or gluten-free all-purpose flour
+ ¼ cup (59 ml) canola oil
+ ¼ cup (20 g) nutritional yeast
+ 2 tablespoons (24 g) taco seasoning, plus more to taste
+ 1 teaspoon sea salt
+ 3 tablespoons (45 g) tahini
+ 1 tablespoon (15 ml) white wine vinegar
+ 1 tablespoon (15 g) Dijon mustard
+ 2 cups (475 ml) nondairy milk
+ 1 can (10 ounces/280 g) diced tomatoes with green chilies, drained (I prefer Rotel brand.)

FOR CHILI-LIME CHIPS:

+ 1 bag (12 ounces/340 g) tortilla chips
+ 1 teaspoon chili powder, plus more to taste
+ 1 lime, halved

To make the queso:
Add the flour and canola oil to a saucepan over medium heat. Whisk continuously until the mixture is creamy and smooth and thickens just slightly. Lower the heat and add the nutritional yeast, taco seasoning, salt, tahini, vinegar, and Dijon. Whisk until well combined. Add the milk and whisk to combine everything until you have a faint orange-colored queso. Add the tomatoes and mix until well combined. Bring the queso to a bubble, then lower the heat to a simmer for a few minutes just to blend the flavors, stirring frequently to avoid sticking to the pan.

To make the chili-lime chips:
Preheat the oven to 350°F (175°C, or gas mark 4). Line a large sheet pan with parchment paper. Arrange the bag of tortilla chips in a single layer and sprinkle with chili powder, to taste. Squeeze the lime halves over the chips, getting lime juice on as many pieces as you can. Bake for 6 to 8 minutes, or until the chips have browned slightly and the lime juice dries.

Serve the warm queso with chips. To reheat the queso, set it over low heat until warmed throughout. This will keep in the refrigerator for up to 1 week.

YIELD 6 to 8 servings

TIP

For a heartier queso, omit half of the tomatoes and add ½ cup (50 g) vegan sausage or chorizo roughly chopped or crumbled.

BAKED THAI CHILI CAULIFLOWER BITES

When you watch the Vancouver, British Columbia, episode of *The Vegan Roadie*, you'll see we went to a restaurant called Meet on Main. They have a very popular Sweet Thai Chili Cauliflower Bites appetizer on their menu. I couldn't resist re-creating a version for this book! These hit the spot with a combination of the heat and the sweet. These bites also cut calories a bit as they are baked and not fried. It's always a home run in my cooking classes.

+ ¼ cup (38 g) dark brown sugar
+ 1 tablespoon (15 ml) chili garlic sauce
+ 1 tablespoon (20 g) maple syrup
+ 1 tablespoon (15 ml) toasted sesame oil
+ 2 tablespoons (28 ml) soy sauce or gluten-free tamari
+ ¼ teaspoon ginger powder
+ ½ cup (25 g) panko or gluten-free panko bread crumbs
+ ¼ cup (35 g) yellow stone-ground cornmeal
+ 2 tablespoons (16 g) white sesame seeds, plus more for sprinkling
+ 4 cups (528 g) cauliflower, cut into small bite-size florets
+ Cooking spray
+ 2 scallions, thinly sliced
+ Coco Loco peanut sauce (page 154, optional)

Preheat the oven to 400°F (200°C, or gas mark 6). Line a large sheet pan with parchment paper.

In a large bowl, combine the sugar, chili garlic sauce, maple syrup, sesame oil, soy sauce, and ginger. Whisk until well combined.

In a separate bowl combine the panko, cornmeal, and sesame seeds. Mix until well combined.

Add the cauliflower to the bowl with the sauce and toss until well combined, getting the sauce into the nooks and crannies of the cauliflower florets. Add one-third of the dry bread crumb mixture and toss to combine. Add half the remaining crumbs and toss again to combine. Add the remaining crumbs and toss until cauliflower is evenly coated.

Spray the prepared sheet pan with cooking spray, transfer the coated cauliflower bites to the tray, and spray the bites lightly with the cooking spray. Bake for 15 minutes, flip the cauliflower pieces, and bake for 15 minutes, until they start to brown and crisp.

Transfer to a serving dish and sprinkle with scallions and sesame seeds. Serve with Coco Loco peanut sauce (if using).

YIELD 4 to 6 servings

TIP

Hold on to the white parts of the scallions and the stalks and leaves of the cauliflower for making Scrappy Veggie Broth (page 35). You can also chop up the white parts of scallions and store in the refrigerator to sprinkle on salads or literally any main dish you want to give a little extra panache.

LOADED SHEET-PAN NACHOS

Nachos are EVERYTHING! Am I right?! The creative part of making nachos is my favorite part. Tortilla chips are like a blank canvas to carry bite-size parcels of food to your food trap (aka mouth). Make this recipe first as is, and then come back to it and omit ingredients you don't like or add your favorites! As long as it's slathered with some cheese at the end, you can't go wrong.

+ 1 bag (12 ounces/340 g) tortilla chips
+ 1 cup (70 g) shredded red cabbage
+ 1 can (15 ounces/425 g) black beans, drained and rinsed
+ ½ cup (82 g) frozen or fresh corn
+ ½ red bell pepper, roughly chopped
+ 1 can (2.25 ounces/64 g) sliced black olives, drained
+ 1 cup (115 g) vegan cheese shreds or (215 g) Punk Cheddah sauce (page 157)
+ 1 cup (260 g) store-bought salsa
+ 1 avocado, peeled and chopped (optional)
+ Vegan sour cream or 3-Minute Cashew Cream Sauce (page 33, optional)
+ Sliced jalapeños, can, jar, or fresh (optional)
+ 3 scallions, roughly chopped

Preheat the oven to 400°F (200°C, or gas mark 6). Line a 11 x 16–inch (28 x 41–cm) rimmed sheet pan with parchment paper.

Spread a single layer of tortilla chips over the entire sheet pan. Evenly disperse the cabbage, black beans, corn, bell pepper, and black olives until the tortilla chips are completely covered. Sprinkle or drizzle cheese over the top.

Bake the nachos for 10 to 12 minutes, or until the cheese is melted and the edges of the chips on the outside of the sheet pan have just browned. Be careful not to burn the tortilla chips. Some store-bought vegan cheeses can be finicky. If needed, turn the oven up to broil for just 1 to 2 minutes to give the cheese that little extra push to melt.

Remove the nachos from the oven and top with salsa, avocado, sour cream, and jalapeños (if using). Sprinkle with scallions and serve directly from the sheet pan. Warn your guests that the sheet pan is hot.

YIELD 6 to 8 servings

TIP

Not making this for a party? Split the recipe in half for a smaller crowd or dinner for two, easy peasy. Use the tops and the insides of the pepper (seeds and core) to make Scrappy Veggie Broth (page 35). You can freeze the pepper scraps and use them when you are ready!

STOVE TOP MOVIE THEATER POPCORN

Please stop buying that crusty, stale microwave popcorn. You can make a delicious, personally crafted, salty, crunchy, warm bowl of popcorn yourself to enjoy for that *Vegan Roadie* marathon I know you are about to start! Not only that, a freshly made stove top pot of popcorn has a 98.8 percent success rate of getting a potential suitor's attention. When used appropriately, it has an 83 percent rate of return on a dinner invitation. Yes, it is the food equivalent to the bend and snap from *Legally Blonde*, "works every time." Promise.

+ ½ cup (105 g) corn kernels
+ ¼ cup (59 ml) canola or neutral oil of choice
+ ½ teaspoon sea salt, plus more to taste

Combine the corn kernels, oil, and salt in a medium saucepan. Cover and heat over medium-high heat. When kernels start to pop, shake the pot back and forth while still over the heat until the popcorn begins to rapidly pop.

Once the popcorn has filled the pot three-quarters of the way, turn off the heat. Let it sit, covered, for 1 minute or until it has finished popping. Transfer to a large bowl and adjust the salt if desired.

YIELD 4 servings

TIP

Make this ahead of time and store in an airtight container for up to 1 week. Have it as a snack when desired. While it won't be as crunchy as it is when freshly made, it will still be delicious. Resealable baggies are perfect for sneaking it into a movie theater . . . just sayin'.

SIMPLE SOUTHWEST QUESADILLA WITH PINEAPPLE DREAM SAUCE

Back in my days as a server at a place called Bennigan's, they had these Southwest eggrolls with creamy pineapple dipping sauce that my sister was bananas for. So, this is for my sister, a much easier version to make combining vegan cheese, crispy vegetables, and optional tofu, seitan, or vegan chicken on corn tortillas baked in the oven all at once. No frying required. Serve it up with plain salsa or go the extra mile and make this decadent, easy pineapple dipping sauce to wow your in-laws or whomever.

FOR SOUTHWEST QUESADILLA:

+ 12 (6-inch/15-cm) corn tortillas
+ 1 red bell pepper, roughly chopped
+ ½ red onion, roughly chopped
+ 1 cup (164 g) fresh or frozen corn
+ 1¼ cups (135 g) vegan cheddar shreds
+ 2 teaspoons (4 g) ground cumin
+ 2 teaspoons (4 g) chili powder
+ 1 teaspoon sea salt, plus more for sprinkling
+ Cooking spray
+ Chopped fresh cilantro (optional)

FOR CREAMY PINEAPPLE DREAM SAUCE:

+ ½ cup (115 g) vegan mayonnaise
+ 2 tablespoons (33 g) store-bought salsa of choice
+ 3 tablespoons (32 g) canned crushed pineapple, drained with liquid reserved

Preheat the oven to 400°F (200°C, or gas mark 6). Line a large sheet pan with parchment paper.

To make the Southwest quesadilla:
Add the bell pepper, onion, corn, cheese, cumin, chili powder, and salt to a bowl. Toss to combine. Lay 6 corn tortillas on the sheet pan. Add ½ cup (120 ml) scoop of the mixture to each tortilla and top with the remaining 6 corn tortillas.

Spray the tortillas lightly with cooking spray and sprinkle with a touch more salt, if desired. Bake for 10 minutes and then flip each quesadilla. Spray again lightly with cooking spray and sprinkle sparingly with salt if desired. Bake for 10 minutes, until golden brown and cheese has melted.

To make the creamy pineapple dream sauce:
Mix the mayonnaise, salsa, and pineapple in a bowl until well combined.

Remove the quesadillas from the oven and sprinkle with cilantro (if using). Cut each one into quarters, 4 triangles. Transfer to a serving plate, and serve with pineapple dream sauce or salsa of choice.

YIELD 6 quesadillas

TIP

This is a fast and efficient hot app to serve at parties. When they come out of the oven, cut each quesadilla into 4 pieces. Place the sauce in a bowl in the middle of a round serving platter and then fan the quesadilla pieces out around the sauce. Sprinkle the quesadilla pieces with freshly chopped cilantro for a little extra flare.

MADE IN MINUTES MINI PIZZA CUPS

I love cheese pizza. It might be the actual reason I moved to New York City when I was eighteen. Just to get that dollar slice! As time has passed and the dollar slice is no longer an option, I have crafted my love of the cheese pizza. For this version, I offer options to make it deluxe or feel free to stay as basic as you wish to get it done in minutes. It's your call. Either way you will be left with some crunchy thin-crust mini bites of cheese pizza goodness for your guests, or just yourself if you're not one to share your pizza. I always have intentions to share buuuuttttt . . .

+ Cooking spray
+ 2 large (10-inch/25-cm) flour tortillas
+ ¾ cup (183 g) canned or jarred pizza sauce
+ ¾ cups (86 g) vegan mozzarella shreds
+ Italian seasoning (optional)
+ Toppings of choice (optional)

Preheat the oven to 425°F (220°C, or gas mark 7). Lightly spray a 12-cavity muffin tin with cooking spray.

Use a 3-inch (7.5-cm) biscuit cutter or the top of the can of pizza sauce to cut 6 rounds from each tortilla. If using the can, empty the sauce into a bowl and wash the can before using it to cut the rounds. Save the tortilla scraps to make tortilla crisps (see tip).

Gently push each tortilla round into a cavity in the muffin tin creating a shallow bowl. Lightly spray the rounds with cooking spray. Place 1 tablespoon (15 ml) of sauce on each round and top with 1 tablespoon (7 g) of cheese. Sprinkle with Italian seasoning and toppings of choice (if using).

Bake for 10 to 12 minutes, until the cheese has melted and the sides of the tortilla rounds have started to brown. Pop the pizzas out of the cavities with a fork and serve warm.

YIELD 12 pizza cups

TIP

I'm a saucy guy, so I put 1 tablespoon (15 ml) of sauce on each round. If you aren't the saucy type, adjust to your liking and start with 1 to 2 teaspoons of sauce. To use the tortilla scraps, heat 2 tablespoons (30 ml) of canola or neutral oil in a medium skillet and add the tortilla scraps. Quickly sprinkle them with sea salt and gently toss to fry all sides. Remove and place on a paper towel to soak up the oil. Eat as a snack or use as a salad topper.

FAST OOEY GOOEY CAST PARTY BEAN DIP

There were a couple of summers in high school when I attended a performing arts camp. Shout out to Trollwood in Fargo, North Dakota. After shows, there was always a cast party, and more often than not, we turned to this old standby because we were kids and it was easy. It's essentially a queso in layers. With the influx of vegan products available on the market, I couldn't resist the chance to veganize it for this book. Traditionally it was made in the microwave, but I find with its vegan counterparts for ingredients, it's best to use the oven to whip up this very satisfying, melted, ooey gooey conglomeration of now-easy-to-find pantry items. Though I do offer an optional scallion garnish here, my sixteen-year-old self wasn't that bougie after tapping my way through a night of *42nd Street*. It's fine to go without scallions. You do you.

+ 1 container (8 ounces/225 g) vegan cream cheese, room temperature

+ 1 can (14.5 ounces/411 g) vegan chili

+ 1 cup (115 g) vegan cheddar shreds

+ 2 scallions, thinly sliced (optional)

+ Tortilla chips

Preheat the oven to 375°F (190°C, or gas mark 5).

In an 8 x 8–inch (20 x 20–cm) baking dish, spread the cream cheese in a single layer, top with chili, and then finish with cheddar shreds. Bake for 14 to 16 minutes, until the cheese has melted and edges are bubbly.

Remove from the oven and let cool for at least 5 minutes or you will absolutely burn the roof of your mouth upon first bite. Sprinkle with scallions (if using), and serve with tortilla chips for dipping.

YIELD 8 servings

TIP

Get fancy! This recipe started as a basic betty and as an adult I added scallions to it . . . but don't stop there! This could easily become your 32-layer dip. Add jalapeños, avocado, sliced black olives, shredded cabbage, lettuce, and so on. This baking dish is a fiesta just waiting to happen. But if your endgame is a melting pot of hearty goodness to quickly satisfy guests at a party, make it as is and I promise you the baking dish will be licked clean.

MISO-GARLIC CHEESE BREAD

This is an amped-up version of the frozen garlic bread from the supermarket. For me it screams perfection from the first bite of its flaky crispy crust down to its melty buttery chew. Make it as is and then create your own variations to suit your taste!

+ ¼ cup (55 g) vegan butter, soft at room temperature
+ 1 tablespoon (16 g) miso
+ 1 tablespoon (5 g) nutritional yeast
+ 1 teaspoon garlic powder
+ 1 (12-inch/30-cm) baguette, halved and scored into 12 pieces, 24 pieces total (see tip)
+ ½ cup (57 g) vegan mozzarella shreds, plus more to taste
+ ½ teaspoon Italian seasoning
+ Crushed red pepper (optional)

Preheat the broiler in the oven. DO NOT line a sheet pan with parchment paper.

In a small bowl, cream together the butter, miso, nutritional yeast, and garlic powder until well combined.

Lay each side of the baguette on a sheet pan with the scored insides facing up. Spread the mixture on the baguettes, dividing the mixture evenly between the 2 pieces. Sprinkle each one with ¼ cup (26 g) mozzarella shreds. Add more shreds if desired. Finish by sprinkling each baguette with ¼ teaspoon Italian seasoning and the desired amount of crushed red pepper (if using).

Place in the broiler for 3 minutes. Rotate the pan and broil for another 3 minutes, until the butter mixture underneath the cheese browns and the cheese has melted. Remove from the oven and briefly let cool to the touch before breaking pieces off and transferring them to a serving platter or plate.

Remember, all broilers have different intensity. Keep an eye on the bread. If you find after the first 3 minutes the butter has browned and the cheese is melted, there is no need to continue broiling.

YIELD 24 pieces

TIP

Traditionally bread is scored before it's baked to allow it to expand during baking. Here, we are scoring it to precut the bread into pieces so you can easily pull pieces apart after baking. Start this recipe by cutting the 12-inch (30-cm) baguette in half lengthwise and placing the outside of the baguettes on a flat surface. Use a sharp knife to slice into the bread, but don't slice all the way through when you reach the bottom, leaving just the outer crust connected. Pieces should be 1 inch (2.5 cm) long creating 12 pieces in each side of the baguette for a total of 24 pieces.

CHAPTER FOUR

SOUPS 'N SUCH: LET'S GIVE THEM SOMETHING TO STEW ABOUT!

VERY FAST VEGGIE LENTIL SOUP

Lentils are packed with protein, and vegetables are packed with nutrients. Put them together in a soup and pair it with a delicious grain bowl or salad for lunch and you are set! The creamy texture of the lentils with the soft crunch of freshly cooked vegetables is a surefire delight, especially when mixed with some robust diced tomatoes. I love making this soup for meal prep and pairing it with the Lemon and Garlic and Thyme, Oh My! (page 137) or Italian Cheesy Herbed Tofu and Kale Bowl (page 123).

+ 1 tablespoon (15 ml) olive oil

+ 1 onion, diced

+ 2 celery stalks, thinly sliced

+ 2 carrots, peeled and thinly sliced

+ 4 cloves garlic, minced

+ 6 cups (1.4 L) vegetable broth or Scrappy Veggie Broth (page 35)

+ 1 russet potato, skin on, cut into ½-inch (1-cm) cubes

+ 1 cup (164 g) frozen or fresh corn

+ 1 head broccoli (about 3 cups/ 200 g) cut into tiny florets

+ 2 (15 ounces/425 g) cans brown lentils, drained and rinsed

+ 1 can (14.5 ounces/411 g) diced tomatoes, with juices

+ 1½ cups (100 g) kale, roughly chopped into small pieces

+ 1 teaspoon dried oregano

+ 1 teaspoon sea salt

+ ½ teaspoon black pepper

In a large stockpot, heat the oil over medium heat. Add the onion, celery, and carrots. Sauté for 3 minutes, until the onions are soft. Add the garlic and sauté for 1 minute, until fragrant.

Add the broth and potato, cover, and bring to a boil. Reduce to a simmer and continue to cook, covered, for 6 to 8 minutes, until the potatoes are fork-tender. Add the corn, broccoli, lentils, tomatoes, kale, oregano, salt, and pepper. Let simmer for 2 to 4 minutes, covered until the broccoli has become fork-tender.

YIELD 6 to 8 servings

TIP

If you prefer dried lentils to canned lentils, simply cook them according to the package directions. Then add 1½ cups (297 g) cooked lentils in place of the canned.

5-INGREDIENT PASTA FAGIOLI AS SEEN ON *THE VEGAN ROADIE*

Season 3 of *The Vegan Roadie* took us to Italy. We filmed six jam-packed episodes from Sicily to Florence and ate as much as we could manage in between. I was never a fan of pasta fagioli; that was of course until I made it alongside Rosario Maria at a little restaurant called Tubba Catubba in Naples. So simple, yet so flavorful. If you have a garden and you grow tomatoes, this is the soup for you! But don't let not having a garden stop you from making this easy and satisfying soup. I like to toss this on the stove on a busy weeknight, especially when I have a pint of cherry tomatoes I'm worried might go bad. This uses them up in a cinch, providing a soup you can enjoy for the next few days.

+ 2 cloves garlic, halved
+ 4 cups (940 ml) vegetable broth or Scrappy Veggie Broth (page 35)
+ 1 pint (474 g) cherry tomatoes, halved
+ 1 can (15 ounces/425 g) cannellini beans, drained and rinsed
+ 1 cup (120 g) ditalini or macaroni pasta
+ 1 tablespoon (16 g) tomato paste
+ ½ teaspoon sea salt, plus more for seasoning
+ Olive oil (optional)
+ Fresh basil leaves (optional)

Add the garlic and broth to a stockpot. Bring to a boil and then reduce to a simmer for 3 minutes. Add the cherry tomatoes, beans, and pasta. Let the pasta cook according to package directions until al dente, about 8 to 10 minutes. Add the tomato paste and salt, then stir to combine. Add salt to taste. Remove the garlic.

Transfer to serving bowls, and garnish with a drizzle of olive oil and a basil leaf (if using).

YIELD 4 servings

TIP

You might be tempted to mince the garlic, but don't do it! Italians traditionally cook garlic whole and pull it out before serving. I halved the garlic because I found it difficult to fight the urge not to mince it, so this is my compromise!

CREAMY CHICKPEA POTPIE SOUP

Potpies are awesome: flaky crust bursting with creamy filling and delicious vegetables. But flaky store-bought vegan pastry crust is not always easy to come by, yet. It never hurt nobody to cut some carbs from their dinner, so I put together this soup so I could have the nostalgic savory flavors served up in a flash in the convenience of a bowl. No baking required. Unless you want to serve this with a side of Effortless Buttered Pan Biscuits (page 44), which I highly recommend if you like bread with your soup.

+ 2 tablespoons (30 ml) olive oil (optional)
+ 1 onion, chopped
+ 2 carrots, thinly sliced
+ 2 celery ribs, thinly sliced
+ 4 cloves garlic, minced
+ 2 russet potatoes, skin on and diced small
+ 5 cups (1.2 L) vegetable broth or Scrappy Veggie Broth (page 35), divided
+ 1 cup (137 g) raw cashews, soaked in water overnight or boiled for 10 minutes in water and drained
+ 1½ teaspoons poultry seasoning
+ 1½ teaspoons sea salt, plus more for seasoning
+ 1 cup (150 g) frozen peas
+ 1 cup (164 g) frozen corn
+ 1 can (15 ounces/425 g) chickpeas, drained and rinsed
+ 1 teaspoon black pepper, plus more for seasoning
+ 1 tablespoon (15 ml) apple cider vinegar
+ Scallions or chives, roughly chopped (optional)

Heat the oil (if using) in a stockpot over medium heat. Add the onion, carrots, and celery and sauté for 3 to 5 minutes, until the onions are soft and translucent. Add the garlic and sauté for 1 minute, until fragrant.

Add the potatoes and 4 cups (940 ml) of broth to the pot. Cover and bring to a boil. Reduce to a simmer and cook, covered, for 8 to 10 minutes, until the potatoes are just fork-tender. Be careful not to let them turn to mush.

While soup is simmering, add the remaining broth, cashews, poultry seasoning, and salt to a blender. Blend for 1 to 2 minutes, until smooth and creamy. Transfer cream to the pot.

Add the peas, corn, chickpeas, pepper, and vinegar to the pot and stir until well combined. Bring to a simmer for 4 minutes to heat everything throughout. Season with salt and pepper to taste.

Serve hot garnished with scallions (if using).

YIELD 24 pieces

TIP

If managing a nut allergy, omit the cashews. Add ¼ cup (32 g) cornstarch to the blender in place of the cashews and blend as directed. Use this as the cream. After adding to the pot, let simmer 4 to 6 minutes, until slightly thicker. This won't be as creamy as the cashew cream, but it will still give you a luscious and silky texture.

BEEFLESS RED WINE STEW

I loved beef stew when I was a kid. My parents were divorced, and my dad wasn't exactly in line to compete on Food Network's *Chopped*. This meant the weekends often consisted of quick processed foods, such as canned beef stew and prepackaged deli meats, that we could pick up at the grocery store on the way to his house. While you won't find those items in my shopping cart anymore, I can appreciate the comfort a hearty beefless stew can bring during cold months.

+ 2 tablespoons (30 ml) olive oil
+ 1 onion, diced
+ 2 carrots, peeled and thinly sliced
+ 2 celery stalks, thinly sliced
+ 2 cups (220 g) vegan beef tips or seitan, chopped or cubed
+ 4 cloves garlic, minced
+ ½ cup (120 ml) red wine
+ 1 russet potato, skin on, cut into ½-inch (1-cm) chunks
+ 3 cups (705 ml) vegetable broth or Scrappy Veggie Broth (page 35)
+ ¼ cup (64 g) tomato paste
+ 2 tablespoons (28 ml) soy sauce or gluten-free tamari
+ ½ teaspoon sea salt
+ ¼ teaspoon black pepper
+ 2 tablespoons (16 g) cornstarch
+ ¼ cup (60 ml) water
+ Chopped fresh parsley (optional)

Heat the oil in a large stockpot over medium heat. Add the onion, carrots, celery, and vegan beef tips. Sauté for 3 minutes, until the onions are soft. Add the garlic and sauté for 1 minute, until fragrant. Add the wine and cook for about 4 minutes, until the wine has evaporated.

Add the potato and vegetable broth and mix until well combined. Bring to a boil and reduce to a simmer. Cover and let cook for 6 to 8 minutes, until the potatoes are fork-tender. Add the tomato paste, soy sauce, salt, and pepper, and mix until incorporated.

In a small bowl, whisk together the cornstarch and water until there are no lumps. Pour the mixture into the stew and mix in until well combined. Let simmer for 4 to 6 minutes, uncovered, until slightly thicker. Serve sprinkled with parsley (if using).

YIELD 6 servings

TIP

Make this veggie-full by omitting the vegan beef tips or seitan and using sliced portobello mushrooms or cremini mushrooms. Simply cook it in place of the beef tips as directed with the onion, carrots, and celery.

MINDFUL MUSHROOM AND CORN CHOWDER

This soup is full of fresh flavor from the array of vegetables, and it's bursting with that hearty umami satisfaction from the cremini mushrooms. It will warm you up on a cold day and is perfect to have on hand in the refrigerator for a quick dinner paired with a simple side salad. It's very satisfying.

+ 2 tablespoons (30 ml) olive oil
+ 1 onion, chopped
+ 4 cloves garlic, minced
+ 2 carrots, peeled and thinly sliced
+ 2 ribs celery, chopped
+ 8 ounces (225 g) sliced cremini or white mushrooms
+ 2 tablespoons (32 g) tomato paste
+ 2 russet potatoes, skin on, cut into ½-inch (1-cm) cubes
+ 4 cups (940 ml) vegetable broth or Scrappy Veggie Broth (page 35)
+ ¾ cup (103 g) raw cashews, soaked in water overnight or boiled for 10 minutes in water and drained
+ 1 cup (235 ml) water
+ 1½ cups (246 g) frozen or fresh corn
+ 2 teaspoons (5 g) Old Bay Seasoning
+ 1½ teaspoons sea salt, plus more for seasoning
+ ½ teaspoon black pepper
+ Juice of ½ lemon
+ Chives, chopped (optional)
+ Oyster crackers (optional)

Heat the oil in a large stockpot over medium heat. Add the onion, garlic, carrots, celery, and cremini. Sauté for 4 to 6 minutes, until the onions are soft and the mushrooms have reduced in size.

Add the tomato paste and stir it into the vegetables, coating them. Add the potatoes and broth. Bring to a boil and cover. Reduce to a simmer and cook for 6 to 8 minutes, until the potatoes are fork-tender.

Add the cashews and water to a blender and blend for 1 to 2 minutes, until smooth and creamy. Add the cashew cream, corn, Old Bay, salt, pepper, and lemon juice to the stockpot. Stir until well combined.

Bring the soup to a simmer for 4 to 6 minutes, until thickened and creamy. Add salt to taste, if desired. Serve garnished with chives on top and oyster crackers on the side (if using).

YIELD 6 servings

TIP

That pesky leftover tomato paste gets me every time. Even though it's a small can, there is always some left. I like to remove the leftover tomato paste by either the teaspoon or tablespoon and portion out into an airtight container and keep in the freezer for up to 4 months. I use the portioned tomato paste as needed and avoid the waste! The trick is remembering I have some in the freezer when I need it.

SAY CHEESE!... AND BROCCOLI SOUP

Omigourd, cheddar broccoli soup: Who doesn't love this combination of creamy warm comfort with a dose of daily vegetables?! This luscious cheese sauce is the perfect vehicle to get any kiddo or adult eating their broccoli. I love to make this on a Sunday and have it waiting for me for dinner throughout the week for a quick go-to when I get home from a long day of work. I often serve it up with a quick green salad and feel like I did the right thing for my body! Really cut the florets into tiny bite-size pieces; two to three florets should fit in a spoonful.

+ 2 cups (475 ml) vegetable broth or Scrappy Veggie Broth (page 35)

+ 4 cups (284 g) broccoli, cut into tiny florets

+ 1 batch Punk Cheddah sauce (page 157)

+ Pumpkin oil or olive oil (optional)

+ Crushed red pepper (optional)

Add the broth to a stockpot and bring to a boil. Add the tiny broccoli florets and cover the pot. Continue to boil for 3 to 4 minutes, until the broccoli is fork-tender. Add the cheese sauce and mix until well combined. Let simmer for 4 minutes, until the soup is heated through.

Serve warm drizzled with oil and sprinkled with a pinch of crushed red pepper (if using).

YIELD 8 servings

TIP

This also makes a quick and easy go-to baked potato topping. Add a couple hearty spoonfuls over a freshly baked potato topped with some store-bought vegan bacon or tempeh bacon crumbles (page 25) and chopped scallions. To bake the perfect potato, preheat the oven to 350°F (175°C, or gas mark 4). Line a sheet pan with parchment paper. Poke a potato all over 8 to 12 times deeply with a fork, coat lightly with olive oil, and sprinkle with salt and pepper. Transfer to a prepared sheet pan and bake for 1 hour, until the outside begins to crisp and is easily pierced with a fork. Remove from the oven and let cool until easily handled. Cut in half and serve cut-side up.

MINUTE MADE MISO SOUP

It's no secret. I'm a big fan of miso. It's peppered throughout this book, and I'm unapologetic about it. I strive to create recipes with familiar ingredients for the masses, but this is one ingredient I just feel like everyone should get to know if they haven't yet. What better way than through a healthful and flavorful soup that is widely known and adored? The health benefits of miso are abundant from vitamins and minerals to overall gut health. In other words, a little bit of miso never hurt nobody!

+ 2 tablespoons (30 ml) toasted sesame oil
+ 1 onion, thinly sliced
+ 1 carrot, thinly sliced
+ 2 celery stalks, thinly sliced
+ 5 ounces (140 g) shiitake mushrooms, thinly sliced
+ 1 tablespoon (7 g) fresh ginger, grated or minced
+ 1 sheet (3 g) nori, roughly chopped
+ 6 cups (1.4 L) vegetable broth or Scrappy Veggie Broth (page 35)
+ 1 block (14 ounces/396 g) firm tofu, cut into ½-inch (1-cm) cubes
+ 2 cups (100 g) chopped red, rainbow, or Swiss chard leaves
+ ½ cup (50 g) scallions, thinly sliced, plus more for garnish
+ ½ cup (125 g) white miso
+ 1 cup (235 ml) water
+ Juice of 1 lemon

Heat the oil in a large stockpot over medium heat. Add the onion, carrot, celery, mushrooms, and ginger. Sauté for 4 to 6 minutes, until the vegetables are soft and mushrooms have reduced in size. Stir occasionally to evenly sauté and avoid burning the ginger. Add the nori and mix until well combined.

Slowly add the broth and stir to combine. Bring to a boil and reduce to a simmer. Add the tofu, chard, and scallions. Let simmer for 1 minute, until the greens have wilted.

In a bowl, whisk together the miso and water until the lumps have been worked out. Slowly add the miso-water mixture and lemon juice to the soup. Stir to combine.

Garnish with more scallions when serving, if desired.

YIELD 8 servings

TIP

One of my favorite instructors at the Natural Gourmet Institute, Chef Elliot Prag, made an AMAZING miso soup that had rice vinegar and utilizes kombu, wakame seaweed, and arame seaweed. I wanted to keep this recipe closer to mainstream staple items to make it simple, but if seaweed variations intrigue you, I implore you to Google Chef Elliot's Famous Miso Soup or pick up a copy of the *Natural Gourmet Institute Cookbook* and give his recipe a try!

EASY BLACK BEAN SOUP

This is a simplified variation of a black bean soup I fell in love with when attending the Natural Gourmet Institute in New York City. The final result is comforting, creamy, and perfect for a rainy day. The flavor punch comes with the final addition of seasoned rice vinegar boosting the natural savory flavors with a touch of tang.

+ 2 tablespoons (30 ml) olive oil

+ 1 onion, diced

+ 1 carrot, peeled and thinly sliced

+ 2 celery stalks, thinly sliced

+ 4 cloves garlic, minced

+ 2 (15 ounces/425 g) cans black beans, drained and rinsed, divided

+ ¾ cup (120 g) canned crushed tomatoes

+ 2 cups (475 ml) vegetable broth or Scrappy Veggie Broth (page 35)

+ 1 teaspoon chili powder

+ 1 teaspoon ground cumin

+ 1 teaspoon Italian seasoning

+ 1½ teaspoons sea salt, plus more for seasoning

+ 1 tablespoon (15 ml) seasoned rice vinegar

+ 3-Minute Cashew Cream Sauce (page 33) or vegan sour cream (optional)

+ 4 scallions, thinly sliced (optional)

Heat the oil in a large stockpot. Sauté the onion, carrot, and celery for 3 minutes, until the onions are translucent and soft. Add the garlic and sauté for 1 minute, until fragrant.

Mash one can of the black beans with a fork or potato masher and leave the other can whole. Add the mashed and whole black beans, tomatoes, and vegetable broth, and stir until well combined. Bring to a simmer, cover and let cook for 15 minutes, until the celery and carrots are fork-tender. Add the chili powder, cumin, Italian seasoning, salt, and rice vinegar. Stir until combined. Add salt to taste.

Serve drizzled with cashew cream or sour cream and a sprinkle of scallions (if using).

_____

YIELD 6 servings

TIP

If you prefer freshly cooked black beans to canned, substitute the two cans with 3½ cups (500 g) of cooked Basic Betty Beans (page 21). Freeze any leftover crushed tomatoes and use later for pizza sauce, chili, sloppy joes, meatball simmer sauce, or even a quick individual serving of pasta.

SPICY CHICKPEA ALMOND AND KALE SOUP

I came up with the first version of this recipe in a hotel room while filming the St. Louis episode of *The Vegan Roadie*. This is a straight-to-the-pot, one-and-done type recipe. It was one of the most popular "5 Ingredient Challenges" from the series. After testing it several more times, I added a few more ingredients to really bring the robust flavors home. The creaminess of the almond butter has me coming back for seconds every time! This is also one of those recipes that is excellent for leftovers, getting a little thicker and creamier as it sits overnight.

+ 1 tablespoon (15 ml) toasted sesame oil, plus more for serving
+ ½ onion, diced
+ 1 can (15 ounces/425 g) chickpeas, drained and rinsed, divided
+ ¼ cup (60 ml) garlic chili sauce
+ 2 tablespoons (28 ml) soy sauce or gluten-free tamari
+ 2 cups (475 ml) vegetable broth or Scrappy Veggie Broth (page 35)
+ 2 cups (475 ml) unsweetened soy or almond milk
+ Juice of 1 lime
+ ½ cup (130 g) almond butter
+ 1 teaspoon sea salt
+ 2 cups (134 g) kale, destemmed and chopped into bite-size pieces
+ 3 tablespoons (60 g) maple syrup
+ 4 scallions, thinly sliced (optional)

Heat the oil in a large stockpot. Add the onion and sauté for 3 minutes, until translucent. Divide the chickpeas in half, add the first half to the stockpot, and smash them with a fork or a potato masher.

Add the second half of chickpeas to the pot and keep them whole. Add the garlic chili sauce, soy sauce, vegetable broth, milk, lime juice, almond butter, and salt to the stockpot. Stir until well combined and the almond butter has melted.

Heat over medium-high heat and bring to a boil, and then reduce to a simmer. Add the kale and maple syrup. Continue to simmer for 2 to 4 minutes, until the kale is completely wilted.

Serve drizzled with sesame oil and sprinkled with scallions (if using).

YIELD 4 to 6 servings

TIP

This also makes an excellent ramen broth. Boil a couple of packets of cheap ramen or go authentic with some vegan chuka soba curly noodles found in the international section of the supermarket. Just add the noodles with the kale and simmer for 3 to 6 minutes, until the noodles are done cooking.

SIMPLE SEITAN TIKKA MASALA

I started making this recipe several years ago. Since then, it has gone through many incarnations from just chickpeas to just seitan to using chicken meat alternative, etc. I've settled on this combination of savory, succulent seitan paired with burst-in-your-mouth chickpea goodness. Upton's Naturals is my favorite brand when it comes to store-bought seitan. Housed in a luscious coconut cream sauce, it's become a "lick the bowl clean" sort of recipe in our home!

+ 1 tablespoon (15 ml) olive oil
+ 1 white onion, diced
+ 3 cloves garlic, minced
+ 1½ cups (352 g) seitan, roughly chopped into bite-size pieces
+ 1 can (15 ounces/425 g) chickpeas, drained and rinsed
+ ¾ teaspoon sea salt
+ 1 teaspoon ginger powder
+ 1 teaspoon ground cumin
+ 2 teaspoons (4 g) garam masala
+ 2 tablespoons (32 g) tomato paste
+ 1 can (14.5 ounces/411 g) diced tomatoes, with juices
+ 1 can (13.5 ounces/983 ml) full-fat coconut milk
+ Rice Realness or Cauliflower Rice for the Win (page 20 or page 32, optional)
+ Chopped fresh cilantro (optional)

Heat the oil in a large, deep skillet over medium heat. Add the onion and sauté for 3 minutes, until soft. Add the garlic and sauté for 1 minute, until fragrant. Add the seitan and chickpeas and let cook for 2 to 4 minutes to lightly sear the seitan.

Add the salt, ginger, cumin, and masala, and mix until well combined. Add the tomato paste, tomatoes, and coconut milk. Mix until well combined and bring to a simmer for 4 to 6 minutes, until heated through.

Serve over rice or cauliflower rice sprinkled with fresh cilantro (if using).

YIELD 6 to 8 servings

TIP

One of my favorite ways to use this recipe is atop baked sweet potatoes! Follow instructions for baking a potato in the recipe tip for Say Cheese!... and Broccoli Soup (page 89). Cooking times will vary depending on size of potato. Serve the baked sweet potato on a plate, cut-side up with a generous serving of the Simple Seitan Chickpea Tikka Masala on top.

ZIPPY ZUPPA TOSCANA

This soup is always a crowd-pleaser with the robust sausage flavors and creamy comfort of the potatoes. It's hard not to have seconds and even thirds! Inspired by the Olive Garden soup you thought you could never have again since you went vegan.

+ 2 tablespoons (30 ml) olive oil, plus more for garnish
+ 1 large white onion, diced
+ 4 vegan Italian sausage links, thinly sliced
+ 2 cloves garlic, minced
+ 2 large russet potatoes, sliced in half lengthwise and sliced into ¼-inch (2-cm) slices
+ 6 cups (1.4 L) vegetable broth or Scrappy Veggie Broth (page 35)
+ 2 teaspoons (10 g) sea salt, plus more to taste
+ 1 teaspoon black pepper, plus more to taste
+ 1 teaspoon Italian seasoning
+ 2 tablespoons (16 g) cornstarch or arrowroot
+ ¼ cup (60 ml) water
+ Juice of ½ lemon
+ 3 cups (90 g) baby spinach
+ Crushed red pepper (optional)

Heat the oil in a large stockpot over medium heat. Add the onion and sausage. Sauté for 4 to 6 minutes, until the onions have softened and sausage has slightly browned. Add the garlic and sauté for 1 minute, until fragrant.

Add the potatoes and the vegetable broth and bring to a boil. Cover and reduce to a simmer. Cook for 8 to 10 minutes, until the potatoes are fork-tender. Add the salt, pepper, and Italian seasoning, and mix until well combined.

In a bowl, whisk together the cornstarch and water until lumps have been worked out.

Add the cornstarch mixture to the soup and bring back to a simmer. Add the lemon juice and spinach. Continue to simmer for 4 to 6 minutes, until the soup has slightly thickened and the spinach has completely wilted. Add salt and pepper to taste.

Serve hot, garnished with a drizzle of oil and a sprinkle of crushed red pepper (if using).

YIELD 6 servings

TIP

Elevate this soup by creating a luscious broth. Just add 1 cup (235 ml) of the 3-Minute Cashew Cream Sauce (page 33) after the spinach. With the addition of the cream, it's safe to call it a creamy sausage potato soup—perfect for a bread bowl!

CHAPTER FIVE

IT'S A HANDFUL: SANDWICHES, TACOS, AND BURRITOS THAT PACK A PUNCH

THE COFFEEHOUSE VEGGIE SANDWICH

Gone are the days when you would walk into a coffee shop and the only vegan offering was a bland vegetable sandwich barely held together with some hummus and lettuce. Now coffeehouses and beyond offer a wide variety of vegan savories and sweets, but I'll never forget those veggie sandwiches. I was actually very fond of them (when I would make them myself)! So, this is my version, stepped up a bit with some walnuts and an oil-and-vinegar mix, inspired by a stop in Italy during the filming of season 3 of *The Vegan Roadie: Ciao Italia!* See the tip for some ideas to create your epic.

+ ½ cup (28 g) spring salad mix
+ ¼ teaspoon olive oil
+ ¼ teaspoon balsamic or red wine vinegar
+ Pinch of sea salt
+ Pinch of black pepper
+ 2 tablespoons (30 g) store-bought hummus
+ 2 pieces vegan bread, toasted
+ ¼ red, orange, or yellow bell pepper, thinly sliced
+ 1 heaping tablespoon (15 g) crushed walnuts

+ 2 slices tomato
+ 8 slices cucumber
+ ¼ cup (59 g) shredded carrot
+ ¼ cup (9 g) alfalfa sprouts
+ ½ avocado, peeled and sliced

In a small bowl, toss together the salad mix, olive oil, vinegar, salt, and pepper.

To build the sandwich, spread the hummus on a piece of toast and top with a layer of peppers. Top the salad mix on the peppers and sprinkle the walnuts over the salad mix, pressing slightly into the mix to keep the walnuts from toppling off the mix. Top with tomatoes followed by cucumber, carrot, and sprouts. Spread the avocado slices over the top of the sprouts and top with the remaining piece of toast. Cut in half.

YIELD 1 sandwich

TIP

Add your favorite mix and match of veggies! I like to thinly slice zucchini when they are in season. If I have some baked tofu on hand, I'll add that to the mix, too! You can use any variety of hummus (I love red pepper hummus!) or even switch out the hummus with vegan cream cheese. Play with your food. Have fun with this one and make it your favorite by adding ingredients you love. If you prefer wraps to sandwiches, this is a great one to wrap in a large tortilla for a quick lunch.

STRESS-FREE REUBEN BURGER

When I started filming my series *The Vegan Roadie* in 2014, I learned something very quickly: Every vegan restaurant thinks they make the best nachos, macaroni and cheese, and Reuben. After a while, I started declining these as an option to film because it was just becoming a show about Reubens! That being said, I thought I would bring it back to life in a super simple burger with a tangy Russian dressing–style sauce, zesty sauerkraut, and ooey gooey cheese. My two-step vegan cheese melt procedure will give you the perfect melt every time. I want to clarify that if you can't find swiss, don't stress! Just choose any vegan cheese by the slice you can find and it will still be yummy.

+ ¼ cup (60 g) vegan mayonnaise
+ 2 tablespoons (30 g) ketchup
+ 1 teaspoon prepared vegan horseradish (see tip)
+ 2 vegan burger patties
+ ½ cup (71 g) sauerkraut
+ 2 slices vegan swiss cheese or vegan cheese slices of choice
+ 1 tablespoon (15 ml) water
+ 2 vegan hamburger buns
+ 2 dill pickle spears

In a bowl, combine the mayonnaise, ketchup, and horseradish. Set aside.

Prepare the burger patties according to package directions in a skillet with a fitted lid. When the burgers are fully cooked, top each one with sauerkraut followed by a slice of cheese. With the lid in hand, add water to the skillet and immediately cover to allow steam to build up and melt the cheese. Wait 45 to 60 seconds, until the cheese is fully melted.

Transfer the burgers to bottom buns and top generously with the sauce mixture. Serve on a plate with a pickle on the side.

YIELD 2 burgers

TIP

Sometimes prepared vegan horseradish is hard to find. You can sub it out for equal parts freshly minced ginger! Toast your buns for the best burger (see tip on page 103). To make a more traditional Reuben, use chopped seitan and sear it in a skillet with olive oil and a dash of soy sauce to give it a hearty rich flavor, sprinkled with salt and pepper. Use the cheese, sauerkraut, and sauce as directed above and serve between two slices of toasted rye bread. Don't forget the pickle on the side!

HAWAIIAN TOFU AND PINEAPPLE SANDO

This tofu has that succulent balance of smoky and sweet. It's topped with a super simple slaw with some pineapple chunks for a touch of tang. Colorful, flavorful, and easy to pull together, this is a great sandwich for any day of the week. If you can't find, or don't like ciabatta, use your bread bun or roll of choice.

FOR TOFU:

+ 2 tablespoons (30 ml) olive oil
+ 2 tablespoons (28 ml) soy sauce or gluten-free tamari
+ 1 tablespoon (15 g) Dijon mustard
+ ¼ cup (38 g) dark brown sugar
+ 1 teaspoon smoked paprika
+ 2 teaspoons (5 g) garlic powder
+ 2 teaspoons (5 g) onion powder
+ ½ teaspoon sea salt
+ ¼ teaspoon black pepper
+ 1 block (14 ounces/396 g) extra-firm tofu, cut into 12 slices
+ 4 vegan ciabatta rolls

FOR PINEAPPLE SLAW:

+ ½ cup (85 g) fresh or canned pineapple chunks, drained
+ 1 cup (70 g) shredded red cabbage
+ ¼ cup (60 g) vegan mayonnaise
+ ½ teaspoon apple cider vinegar
+ 2 pinches sea salt

Preheat the oven to 425°F (220°C, or gas mark 7). Line a sheet pan with parchment paper.

To make the tofu:
Combine the olive oil, soy sauce, Dijon mustard, brown sugar, smoked paprika, garlic powder, onion powder, salt, and pepper in a bowl. Lay the slices of tofu out on the prepared sheet pan in one layer and brush each slice of tofu with the mixture. Half of the mixture should remain after brushing one side. If you don't have a pastry brush, use a paper towel to dab the mixture onto the pieces of tofu. Bake for 15 minutes. Remove from the oven, flip, and brush the other side. Bake for 15 minutes, or until darker brown.

To make the pineapple slaw:
While the tofu finishes baking, combine the pineapple, cabbage, mayonnaise, vinegar, and salt in a small bowl. Mix until well combined.

Remove the tofu from the sheet pan. Place 3 slices on the bottom roll and top with one-quarter of the slaw mixture; continue with remaining ciabatta rolls.

YIELD 4 sandwiches

TIP
Toast that bread to take this sandwich to the next level. Spread the inside of the top and bottom of the ciabatta roll with vegan butter and grill facedown on a skillet until light brown and toasted.

ONE-SHEET BBQ MUSHROOM JACK 'N PEACHES SANDWICHES

This is a variation on pulled pork sandwiches with the addition of peaches. Adding peaches to any BBQ situation, or even just eating BBQ peaches, is delicious! The sweetness paired with the spices of the BBQ sauce make for a super tasty flavor combo. Mix that up with savory and chewy mushrooms and jackfruit and it's a sandwich that even your nonvegan friends will be asking you to make every Fourth of July! Speaking of which, you can turn this into sliders with smaller buns for a breezy appetizer.

+ 8 ounces (225 g) sliced baby bella mushrooms

+ 1 can (14 ounces/396 g) jackfruit, drained and shredded

+ ½ red onion, thinly sliced

+ 1 tablespoon (15 ml) olive oil

+ 1½ cups (243 g) fresh or 1 can (15 ounces/425 g) peaches, drained and roughly chopped

+ ½ teaspoon sea salt

+ ¼ cup (38 g) dark brown sugar

+ ¾ cup (175 ml) vegan BBQ sauce

+ 6 vegan hamburger buns or sandwich rolls

+ 1 cup (235 g) store-bought fried onions

Preheat the oven to 425°F (220°C, or gas mark 7). Line a sheet pan with parchment paper.

Add the mushrooms, jackfruit, and onion to the prepared sheet pan. Drizzle with olive oil and toss to combine. Move everything to one side of the sheet pan. Place the peaches on the cleared side in one layer. Bake for 15 minutes, until the mushrooms have started to reduce in size.

Remove from the oven and add the salt, brown sugar, and BBQ sauce to the jackfruit and mushrooms. Toss to coat jackfruit and mushrooms. Bake for 15 minutes, until the peaches have shrunk slightly and BBQ sauce has evaporated some and become darker in color.

Mix the peaches with the jackfruit mixture. Divide the mixture among 6 bottom buns and top each with fried onions. Add the top bun and enjoy!

YIELD 6 sandwiches

TIP

Toast the buns to level this sandwich up (see tip on page 103). Switch out the peaches with pineapple for a tangier fruit twist. You can also caramelize peaches or pineapple by setting them in a skillet for 6 to 8 minutes over medium-high heat. Flip until the second side is browned and cook for another 6 to 8 minutes.

EASY PEASY OLIVE BURGER

This burger is inspired by a fast-food joint called Hot 'N Now that was popular in my hometown: Saginaw, Michigan. Well, I don't know about popular, but I know when life got busy and I begged enough, my mother would hit up the drive-through. This is a take on their Olive Burger, which I enjoyed too many times to count. In this version, we have tangy olives atop a plant-based burger and melted cheese with creamy vegan mayonnaise. You'll see, it's addictive; if you like olives that is. I'm assuming you do, or you wouldn't have read this far.

+ 2 vegan burgers
+ ¼ cup (32 g) green olives, sliced
+ 2 slices vegan cheese, cheddar, provolone, or mozzarella
+ 1 tablespoon (15 ml) water
+ 2 vegan hamburger buns
+ ¼ cup (14 g) shredded romaine or iceberg lettuce
+ 4 slices tomato
+ 2 tablespoons (30 g) vegan mayonnaise

Cook the burgers according to package directions, using a skillet with a fitted lid. Top each cooked burger with 2 tablespoons (16 g) of olives and a slice of cheese. With the lid in hand, add the water to the skillet and quickly cover to create steam and melt the cheese. Leave the lid on for 45 to 60 seconds, until the cheese has completely melted.

Divide the lettuce between the 2 bottom buns. Top the lettuce with 2 tomato slices. Transfer the burgers and place them atop the tomatoes. Spread 1 tablespoon (15 g) of mayonnaise on top of each bun and top the burger.

YIELD 2 burgers

TIP

Wanna get fancy? Okay, I see you, Martha. Try this with kalamata olives and sautéed shiitake mushrooms with swiss or provolone vegan cheese. Don't forget to toast the buns for that restaurant touch (see tip on page 103.)

DELI DELUXE ITALIAN HOAGIE

Who needs Subway or Jimmy John's when you can build your own massive sandwich at home stacked high with vegan cheeses and meats and topped with veggies tossed in the classic combo of oil and vinegar? Nobody! You got all you need to keep your hands and mouth full right here. Bless the progress of vegan products. These are great to wrap up in parchment paper and take on road trips or a picnic with vegans or nonvegans.

+ 2 cups (110 g) romaine salad mix, from a bag
+ 2 teaspoons (10 ml) olive oil
+ 2 teaspoons (10 ml) red wine vinegar
+ 2 pinches sea salt, or to taste
+ 1 pinch black pepper, or to taste
+ 2 (6-inch/15-cm) vegan hoagie rolls or soft Italian bread
+ ¼ cup (60 g) vegan mayonnaise
+ 4 slices vegan provolone cheese or cheese of choice
+ 8 vegan deli ham slices
+ 8 vegan deli turkey slices
+ 1 Roma tomato, sliced into 8 slices
+ Brown deli mustard (optional)

In a bowl, toss the romaine mix with olive oil, red wine vinegar, salt, and pepper.

Open the hoagie rolls and spread 2 tablespoons (30 g) of mayonnaise on the bottom sides. Layer each roll with 2 cheese slices, 4 ham slices, 4 turkey slices, and 4 tomato slices. Top with half of the salad mixture. Top with brown deli mustard (if using).

YIELD 2 hoagies

TIP

Don't get obsessed with having provolone cheese or turkey and ham. Even though vegan products are becoming readily available, sometimes you have to take what you can get. Use the vegan meats and cheeses that are easiest to find, and I promise you it will still taste delicious!

MUSHROOM CARNITAS AND BRUSSELS BURRITO WITH SWEET RED ONION

Mushrooms: If you like them (and I do), you know they are magical. Not *that* kind of magical (get your head out of the gutter). They take on such a rich and deep flavor when tossed with some oil and roasted in the oven, and they make anything they are added to nice and hearty. With the texture of Brussels sprouts and chickpeas and the sweet hint of maple-kissed red onions, this is a very satisfying burrito.

+ 5 ounces (140 g) sliced shiitake mushrooms
+ 1½ cups (135 g) Brussels sprouts, trimmed and roughly chopped
+ ½ cup (120 g) chickpeas, drained and rinsed
+ 2 tablespoons (15 ml) olive oil, divided
+ ½ teaspoon sea salt
+ ¼ teaspoon black pepper
+ ½ red onion, thinly sliced
+ 2 teaspoons (14 g) maple syrup
+ 2 large (10-inch/26-cm) burrito flour tortillas
+ Vegan sour cream or 3-Minute Cashew Cream Sauce (page 33)
+ Sriracha (optional)

Preheat the oven to 400°F (200°C, or gas mark 6). Line a sheet pan with parchment paper.

Add the mushrooms, Brussels sprouts, and chickpeas to one side of the sheet pan. Drizzle with 1 tablespoon (15 ml) olive oil, and sprinkle with salt and pepper. Toss well to combine. Add the onion to the other side of the sheet pan, drizzle with the remaining olive oil, and toss to combine. Bake for 15 minutes and flip the mushroom mixture. Add the maple syrup to the onion and toss to combine. Bake for 15 minutes, until the mushrooms have browned and reduced in size. Remove from the oven and toss everything with a spatula to mix the onions into the mushroom mixture until combined.

Divide the mixture among the 2 tortillas and drizzle with sriracha (if using). Fold the side of the tortilla closest to you over the filling, then tuck in both sides and roll the burrito away from you until completely wrapped.

YIELD 2 burritos

TIP

The tighter the roll, the more intact the ingredients will stay, meaning a less sloppy eating experience. YouTube has great videos for getting your wrap or burrito roll game on right and tight.

EASY 5-ALARM 2-BEAN TACOS

This recipe goes out to Chris Rios of The Vegan Nom in Austin, Texas! When you watch the Austin episode of *The Vegan Roadie*, you will see me try a variety of tacos from the best taco joint EVER . . . The Vegan Nom. With this recipe, I bring together simple sautéed veggies with basic beans and spice them up with chipotle peppers in adobo sauce for that tongue-tastic kick of heat. It's specifically crafted for those seeking heat in their tacos. You can find cans of chipotle peppers in adobo sauce in the international aisle at the supermarket.

+ 1 tablespoon (15 ml) olive oil
+ ½ onion, chopped
+ ½ green bell pepper, chopped
+ 4 cloves garlic, minced
+ 1 chili minced plus 2 tablespoons (30 ml) sauce from canned chipotle in adobe sauce
+ 1 can (14.5 ounces/411 g) diced tomatoes, drained
+ 1 can (15 ounces/425 g) black beans, drained and rinsed
+ 1 can (15 ounces/425 g) red kidney beans, drained and rinsed
+ ½ teaspoon sea salt
+ 8 (6-inch/15-cm) soft corn tortillas
+ Vegan sour cream or 3-Minute Cashew Cream Sauce (page 33, optional)
+ 4 scallions, thinly sliced (optional)

Heat the oil in a medium skillet over medium heat. Add the onion and bell pepper and sauté for 4 minutes, until the onions are soft and translucent. Add the garlic and sauté for 1 minute, until fragrant.

Add the chili, sauce from chilis, tomatoes, black beans, kidney beans, and salt to the skillet. Bring to a simmer and cook for 6 to 8 minutes, stirring frequently, until heated throughout.

Divide the bean mixture among tortillas and top each one with a dollop of sour cream and sprinkle of scallions (if using).

YIELD 8 tacos

TIP

If you like crispy tortillas, use the same skillet to crisp them up before you start making the bean mixture. Heat 1 tablespoon (15 ml) of neutral oil such as canola or vegetable in the skillet and place a tortilla in and fry until the edges just start to brown. Flip to crisp the other side. Continue until all the tortillas are crispy.

SIMPLE SLOPPY TEMPEH AND AVOCADO BURRITOS

Sloppy joes are delicious and fun, but truth be told the mess always bothered me, even in my youth. I get it, sloppy is in the title, but I just couldn't help it. I've rolled the traditional savory flavors of the sloppy joe up in a tortilla and paired it with the creamy luscious texture of avocado for a twist. I also added greens to get some veggies in. I sneak them in wherever I can! This recipe has become one of my favorites. I hope you love it as much as I do.

+ 2 tablespoons (30 ml) olive oil
+ 1 onion, chopped
+ 1 green bell pepper, seeded and chopped
+ 1 package (8 ounces/225 g) tempeh, crumbled
+ 4 cloves garlic, minced
+ 1 cup (235 ml) tomato sauce
+ 1 tablespoon (15 ml) soy sauce or gluten-free tamari
+ 1 tablespoon (10 g) dark brown sugar
+ 1½ teaspoons chili powder
+ 1 teaspoon ground cumin
+ ½ teaspoon sea salt
+ ¼ teaspoon black pepper
+ 4 (10-inch/26-cm) flour tortillas
+ 1 cup (35 g) packed spinach
+ 1 avocado, peeled and sliced

Heat the oil in a medium skillet over medium heat. Add the onion, bell pepper, and tempeh. Sauté for 6 to 8 minutes, until the onion is soft and the tempeh is browned. Add the garlic and sauté for 1 minute, until fragrant.

Add the tomato sauce, soy sauce, brown sugar, chili powder, cumin, salt, and pepper, and mix until well combined. Bring to a simmer and cook for 4 to 6 minutes, until heated throughout.

Divide the spinach among the tortillas and top each one with the tempeh mixture and avocado.

Fold the side of the tortilla closest to you over the filling, then tuck in both sides and roll the burrito away from you until completely wrapped.

YIELD 4 burritos

TIP

Make it a grilled stuffed burrito! Heat a skillet over medium heat, spray with cooking spray, and set a rolled-up burrito (seam side down) in the skillet. Allow it to crisp up for a minute, then gently flip and allow the other side to brown for the grilled stuffed burrito effect.

PAD THAI BURGERS

The vibrant sweet and sour flavors of pad thai have always won me over. This version is most exciting to me because you can eat it with your hands! What a thrill, eh? Not only is this burger delicious, it looks gorgeous and comes together so easily. This recipe goes great with the Coco Loco peanut sauce (page 154). If you don't have any or just don't feel like getting out the blender, you can make my quick peanut sauce (see tip.)

+ ¼ cup (35 g) shredded red cabbage
+ ¼ cup (59 g) shredded carrot
+ ¼ cup (60 ml) quick peanut sauce (see tip) or Coco Loco peanut sauce (page 154)
+ 2 vegan hamburger buns
+ 2 vegan burger patties, cooked
+ Thinly sliced tomato
+ Thinly sliced cucumber
+ ¼ cup (13 g) bean sprouts
+ Sriracha (optional)
+ 2 tablespoons (30 g) peanuts, crushed
+ Lime wedges (optional)

In a bowl, combine the cabbage and carrot with 2 tablespoons (28 ml) peanut sauce. Mix until well combined.

To assemble the burger, divide the peanut slaw between 2 bottom buns. Place the burger on top of the slaw and add the tomato, cucumber, and sprouts. Drizzle the remaining peanut sauce over each burger and add sriracha (if using). Sprinkle each burger with crushed peanuts.

Serve open-faced with a wedge of lime on the side (if using). Squeeze the lime over the burger before placing the top bun on.

YIELD 2 burgers

TIP

If you don't have any leftover Coco Loco peanut sauce or just don't feel like getting out the blender, make a quick peanut sauce by combining ¼ cup (65 g) peanut butter, 3 tablespoons (45 ml) water, 2 teaspoons (10 ml) soy sauce or tamari, 1 teaspoon chili garlic sauce, 1 tablespoon (20 g) maple syrup, juice of ½ lime, and 1 pinch of sea salt in a bowl. Whisk until well combined. Use as directed in the recipe.

CRUNCHY CLT SAMMY

This is a spin on a time-honored classic, the BLT, using the Easiest Carrot Bacon Ever (page 57). While this is straightforward, have fun with it and make it a base for the sandwich of your dreams. Add store-bought vegan deli meats, more vegetables, and other toppings that you love. You can add more depending on the size of carrot bacon. If my slices came from a medium or small carrot, I have even doubled the number of slices on here. Stack 'em if you got 'em!

+ 1 tablespoon (15 g) vegan mayonnaise

+ 2 slices bread of choice, toasted

+ 2 romaine lettuce leaves

+ 4 thin slices tomato

+ 10 pieces Easiest Carrot Bacon Ever (page 57)

+ Sea salt and black pepper

Spread the mayonnaise on one slice of toast and top that with the romaine, tomato, and carrot bacon. Season with salt and pepper to taste. Top with the remaining piece of toast.

YIELD 1 sandwich

TIP

If you have a favorite vegan store-bought bacon you love, now is the time to cook it up and put it to the test in this traditional sandwich. If you are a mayonnaise lover, don't be shy in putting an extra little bit on the top piece of bread, or even some mustard or brown mustard.

BREEZY CAULIFLOWER AND CHORIZO BRUNCH TACOS

This cauliflower sort-of-scramble is a great option if you either don't like tofu or you're just plum sick and tired of tofu scrambles. Zesty chorizo flavors bring this home when topped with salsa, sour cream, and scallions. Be sure to roughly chop the cauliflower florets into small chunks to resemble more of a scramble.

+ 2 cups (264 g) roughly chopped cauliflower florets
+ ½ cup (80 g) roughly chopped red onion
+ 1 tablespoon (15 ml) olive oil
+ 2 tablespoons (10 g) nutritional yeast
+ ½ teaspoon ground cumin
+ ½ teaspoon ground turmeric
+ ½ teaspoon Himalayan black salt (kala namak) (optional)
+ 1½ cups (152 g) vegan chorizo or sausage, crumbled or roughly chopped
+ 6 (6-inch/15-cm) corn tortillas, hard or soft
+ 6 tablespoons (98 g) store-bought salsa
+ 2 tablespoons (28 g) vegan sour cream or 3-Minute Cashew Cream Sauce (page 33)
+ 4 scallions, thinly sliced (optional)

Preheat the oven to 425°F (220°C, or gas mark 7). Line a large sheet pan with parchment paper.

Add the cauliflower florets and the red onion to the sheet pan. Drizzle with the olive oil and sprinkle with nutritional yeast, cumin, turmeric, and black salt. Toss until well combined and the cauliflower has taken on a yellow hue from the turmeric. Bake for 15 minutes, until the cauliflower has reduced slightly in size.

Add the chorizo to the sheet pan and toss until well combined. Bake for 15 minutes, until the cauliflower is slightly charred. Add the tortillas to the top of the mixture, overlapping each other if needed, and let warm in the oven for 2 minutes.

Remove from the oven and build each taco by dividing the mixture among the tortillas. Add salsa and sour cream or cashew cream to each taco, and sprinkle with scallions (if using).

YIELD 6 tacos

TIP

Serve mini tacos as an appetizer at your brunch to get guests talking about how much of a genius you are. You can't help it—you're amazing. To pump up the serving style, cut the edge off the long side of a lime so it sits flat on a surface and then cut one wedge out of the opposite side big enough for a mini taco to sit in. A mini taco sitting in a lime wedge: Lookatchu and your catering skills. It's a super fun serving option for brunch. Pro tip: Mini shells are available for purchase on the interwebs.

CHAPTER SIX

LUNCH BREAK! MEALS ON THE GO FOR THE OFFICE, BREAK ROOM, OR HOME

CRAFTY ONE-POT MAC AND CHEESE

Going vegan means no more boxes with powdered pouches of cheese for easy macaroni and cheese. Or does it? Fortunately, there are a couple of vegan brands on the market these days. But if knowing every ingredient that goes into your system is your thing (applause to you), then this is the mac for you! It's got a healthy dose of miso for gut health, and creamy vegan butter and nutritional yeast bring out the nostalgic cheesy flavors we crave in a mac and cheese.

+ 1 cup (230 g) elbow macaroni or gluten-free elbow macaroni pasta, uncooked
+ 2 tablespoons (28 g) vegan butter
+ 1 tablespoon (16 g) white miso
+ 1 teaspoon Dijon mustard
+ ⅓ cup (80 ml) unsweetened almond or soymilk
+ ¼ cup (20 g) nutritional yeast
+ ½ teaspoon garlic powder
+ ½ teaspoon onion powder
+ ¼ teaspoon ground turmeric

Cook the pasta according to package directions. Drain and leave the pasta in the colander.

Add the butter, miso, and Dijon mustard to the same saucepan. Melt the butter over medium-low and stir with a spatula to work out the lumps of the miso. When the butter has melted completely, add the milk and continue to work out the miso lumps with the heat on low. Once the lumps are worked out, turn off the heat. Add the nutritional yeast, garlic powder, onion powder, and turmeric. Stir until well combined and a smooth sauce forms.

Add the pasta and toss with the sauce until the macaroni is coated.

Divide into 2 bowls and serve.

YIELD 2 servings

TIP

Add your favorite mix-ins to spruce up this easy one-pot dish. I like to add the Quinoa Bacon Bits from the first *Epic Vegan* book. Consider adding vegan hot dogs or broccoli florets for a little boost to satiate as a meal. If you are into spicy food, this is the perfect bowl to drizzle with sriracha. Of course, a pesto mac never hurt anybody. Top it with Presto Pesto (page 50) and Instant Almond Cheese Crumble (page 33) for a deluxe mac.

RAINBOW VEGETABLES AND TOFU SHEET PAN

This is the sheet pan of all sheet-pan meals, so simple and so satisfying! Packed with nutrients, flavor, and textures from a variety of vegetables and the tofu. I love to make this on a Sunday night to have in the refrigerator and use throughout the week. I like it served warm or cold over greens for a quick lunch.

+ 1 medium sweet potato, washed and cut into ½-inch (1-cm) cubes

+ 1 block (14 ounces/396 g) extra-firm tofu, drained and cut into ½-inch (1-cm) cubes

+ 1 tablespoon (15 ml) olive oil, divided

+ 2 cups (312 g) broccoli florets, cut to bite-size pieces

+ 1 red bell pepper, seeds removed and cut into ½-inch (1-cm) pieces

+ 1 yellow squash, halved lengthwise and cut into ½-inch (1-cm) moons

+ Juice of 1 lemon

+ 2 tablespoons (20 g) nutritional yeast

+ 1½ teaspoons Italian seasoning

+ 1 teaspoon onion powder

+ 1 teaspoon garlic powder

+ 1¼ teaspoons sea salt

+ ¾ teaspoon black pepper

+ Salad greens (optional)

+ Quick Quinoa or Rice Realness (both on page 20, optional)

+ Good Goddess Dressing (page 124) or store-bought dressing (optional)

Preheat the oven to 425°F (220°C, or gas mark 7). Line a sheet pan with parchment paper.

Add the sweet potatoes and tofu to the sheet pan and drizzle with 2 teaspoons (10 ml) of olive oil. Mix to coat in oil. Spread in a single layer and bake for 10 minutes.

In a large bowl, add the broccoli, bell pepper, and squash. Drizzle the remaining olive oil and the lemon juice over the vegetable mixture. Sprinkle with nutritional yeast, Italian seasoning, onion powder, garlic powder, salt, and pepper. Toss everything to evenly coat.

Remove the potatoes and tofu from the oven and flip them with a spatula. Add the vegetable mixture to the sheet pan and use a spatula to toss everything together.

Return to the oven and bake for 15 minutes. Flip everything and spread in one layer. Bake for 15 minutes, until the vegetables have slightly reduced in size and the potatoes have started to brown.

Remove from the oven and let cool slightly. Serve atop a bed of greens and quinoa (if using) to create a rainbow bowl, or enjoy warm on its own. Drizzle with Good Goddess Dressing or store-bought dressing of choice (if using).

YIELD 6 servings

TIP

Switch items out as you please: Use russet potatoes instead of sweet potatoes, cauliflower instead of broccoli, or green bell pepper instead of red to create the color and flavor profile you prefer. If you're using cooking spray, use it in this recipe for an even mist of oil on the tofu, sweet potatoes, and vegetables in place of the olive oil.

BAHN MI ARUGULA BOWL

The flavors of a bahn mi are so popular because the worlds of sweet and spicy collide with the zesty pickling flavors. Traditionally the carrots are pickled and daikon is added into the mix. To keep it easy peasy, here I omitted the daikon and added pickled jalapeños. If you want to toss this on some bread for the full bahn mi effect, I suggest a light and airy baguette.

FOR SWEET SRIRACHA DRESSING:

+ ½ cup (115 g) vegan mayonnaise
+ 1 tablespoon (15 ml) sriracha
+ Juice of ½ lime
+ 1 tablespoon (20 g) maple syrup
+ ¼ teaspoon sea salt

FOR BAHN MI BOWL:

+ 1 block (14 ounces/396 g) extra-firm tofu, drained and cut into ½-inch (1-cm) cubes
+ 2 tablespoons (30 ml) toasted sesame oil
+ 2 tablespoons (28 ml) seasoned rice vinegar
+ 2 tablespoons (26 g) organic cane sugar
+ ½ teaspoon sea salt, divided
+ 1 container (5 ounces/145 g) baby arugula
+ 1 cup (235 g) shredded carrot
+ 1 cucumber, thinly sliced
+ ¼ sweet Vidalia onion, thinly sliced
+ ¼ cup (60 g) pickled jalapeños from a jar or fresh thinly sliced jalapeños

+ Chopped fresh cilantro (optional)
+ 4 scallions, thinly sliced
+ 4 lime wedges

To make the sweet sriracha dressing:
Add the mayonnaise, sriracha, lime juice, maple syrup, and ¼ teaspoon salt to a small bowl. Mix until well combined. Set aside.

To make the bahn mi bowls:
Preheat the oven to 425°F (220°C, or gas mark 7) and line a sheet pan with parchment paper. Add the tofu to the sheet pan, drizzle with oil and vinegar, and sprinkle with sugar and salt. Toss everything until well coated and bake for 15 minutes.

Flip and bake for 15 minutes, until lightly starting to brown. Remove from the oven and allow to cool to the touch.

While the tofu is cooling, divide the arugula, carrot, cucumber, and onion among 4 bowls.

Divide the tofu among the 4 bowls and drizzle each bowl with sriracha aioli mixture. Top the bowls with 1 tablespoon (15 g) of pickled jalapeño and cilantro (if using). Sprinkle each bowl with scallions. Serve with a wedge of lime to be squeezed over the top, if desired.

YIELD 4 bowls

TIP
Use thinly sliced fresh jalapeños, if you want a punch of heat. I love this option myself! But paired with the sriracha aioli, sometimes that's too much heat for some. Pick your poison.

ITALIAN CHEESY HERBED TOFU AND KALE BOWL

This tofu is my absolute favorite to have on hand for meal prep. But I promise you, the leftover tofu from this recipe won't hang around long! Zesty from the lemon juice, herby from a blend of Italian seasoning, and salty and nutty from the nutritional yeast baked with a perfect crust, it's irresistible.

FOR ITALIAN CHEESY HERB TOFU:

+ 1 block (14 ounces/396 g) extra-firm tofu, drained, cut into ½-inch (1-cm) cubes
+ 1 tablespoon (15 ml) olive oil
+ Juice of ½ lemon
+ ¼ cup (20 g) nutritional yeast
+ 1½ teaspoons Italian seasoning
+ 1 teaspoon onion powder
+ 1 teaspoon sea salt
+ 1 teaspoon garlic powder
+ ½ teaspoon black pepper

FOR BOWL:

+ 4 cups (268 g) kale, stems removed and cut into bite-size pieces
+ 2 teaspoons (10 ml) olive oil
+ 2 pinches sea salt
+ ½ cup (118g) shredded carrot
+ 1 avocado, peeled, and sliced
+ 1 cup (198 g) canned lentils, drained

+ Good Goddess Dressing (page 124) or store-bought dressing
+ 2 tablespoons (30 g) crushed pecans (optional)
+ 2 tablespoons (12 g) thinly sliced scallions (optional)

Preheat the oven to 425°F (220°C, or gas mark 7). Line a sheet pan with parchment paper.

To make the Italian cheesy herb tofu:
Combine the tofu, oil, lemon juice, nutritional yeast, Italian seasoning, onion powder, salt, garlic powder, and pepper in a bowl. Mix until combined and evenly coated. Transfer the mixture to the prepared sheet pan and bake for 10 minutes. Flip the tofu with a spatula and bake for 10 minutes, until darkened and slightly crisp. Remove from the oven and let cool.

To make the bowls:
Divide the kale into 2 bowls and drizzle each with 1 teaspoon olive oil. Massage the kale until it is dark green and soft. Divide the carrot, avocado, and lentils between the 2 bowls and top with ¼ cup (30 g) baked tofu. Drizzle each bowl with dressing of choice, and sprinkle with pecans and scallions (if using).

YIELD 2 servings

TIP
If you have an air fryer, toss this tofu together in a bowl and air fry at 380°F (193°C) for 8 minutes. Toss and then continue air frying at 380°F (193°C) for 8 minutes, until you have the perfect crispy outside with a little pillow-y puff of tofu in the middle.

GOOD GODDESS CHOPPY SALAD

Once upon a time, I waited tables at a restaurant in NYC where the chef created a new chopped salad every day. I came to LOVE this salad in particular and had it almost every shift for my meal. What I enjoyed the most was the simplicity of the ingredients. It had a lot of crunch with different textures and vibrant flavors from so many components being packed into one bowl! While this recipe calls for plain tofu, I recommend using the Italian Cheesy Herbed Tofu (page 123) for a little extra flavor punch.

FOR GOOD GODDESS DRESSING:

+ ½ cup (120 g) tahini
+ ¼ cup (59 ml) olive oil
+ ¼ cup (60 ml) water, plus more as needed
+ 2 tablespoons (28 ml) apple cider vinegar
+ 2 tablespoons (28 ml) soy sauce or gluten-free tamari
+ Juice of 1 lemon
+ 1 teaspoon garlic powder
+ ½ teaspoon onion powder
+ ½ teaspoon dried parsley

FOR CHOPPY SALAD:

+ 2 cups (110 g) romaine, roughly chopped
+ 2 cups (60 g) baby spinach
+ 1 cup (248 g) extra-firm tofu, drained and cut into ½-inch (1-cm) cubes
+ ½ cup (75 g) grape tomatoes, halved

+ ½ cup (135 g) roughly chopped cucumber
+ ½ cup (118 g) shredded carrot
+ ¼ cup (60 g) walnuts
+ 1 apple (any variety), cored and roughly chopped
+ ¼ cup (32 g) green olives, pitted
+ 2 tablespoons (15 g) dried cranberries or cherries
+ 1 teaspoon hemp seeds

To make the good goddess dressing:
Add the tahini, olive oil, water, vinegar, soy sauce, lemon juice, garlic powder, and onion powder to a blender. Blend for 1 to 2 minutes, until smooth and creamy. Add more water as needed, 1 tablespoon (15 ml) at a time, to reach desired consistency.

Add the dried parsley to the blender and blend for 10 to 15 seconds, until evenly dispersed but specks are still visible.

To make the choppy salad:
Lay the romaine and spinach on a cutting board and chop roughly with a knife until cut into bite-size pieces. Divide the spinach and lettuce mixture into 2 bowls. Lay the tofu, tomatoes, cucumber, carrot, walnuts, apple, and green olives on the same cutting board and chop everything into tiny pieces. Divide the tofu, vegetable, and fruit bits into the 2 bowls over the spinach and lettuce. Toss until well combined.

Sprinkle each bowl with 1 tablespoon (8 g) of dried cranberries or cherries and drizzle each bowl with the desired amount of dressing. Sprinkle ½ teaspoon hemp seeds over each bowl and serve.

YIELD 2 salads

TIP

If making the elements in advance, toss the apple with lemon juice. There will be dressing leftover to use later on this salad or other salads. The dressing will keep for up to 3 weeks in an airtight container in the refrigerator.

OVERSTUFFED AVOCADO BOWLS

Avocados are so delicious with their buttery flavors, hint of nuttiness, and rich, creamy texture. They are the perfect addition to any meal, and in this case … the center of the meal! A good-for-you fat, avocados supply loads of vitamins (C, E, K, and B6), beta-carotene, and omega-3 fatty acids! So, don't shy away from those calories when it comes to the beloved avocado. This is one of the cases where the calories are totally worth it.

+ 3 cups (201 g) kale, stems removed, torn into bite-size pieces
+ 2 teaspoons (10 ml) olive oil
+ 1 teaspoon balsamic vinegar
+ 1 large ripe avocado, halved, peeled with pit removed (see tip)
+ ¼ cup (59 g) cooked Quick Quinoa (page 20)
+ ¼ cup (60 g) hummus
+ ¼ cup (38 g) small-diced yellow bell pepper
+ ¼ cup (35 g) small-diced cucumber
+ ¼ cup (45 g) small-diced tomato
+ 1 tablespoon (15 g) minced red onion
+ Juice of ½ lemon
+ ¼ teaspoon sea salt
+ ¼ teaspoon black pepper
+ Smoked paprika (optional)
+ Pepitas (optional)

Add the kale, oil, and balsamic to a bowl and massage the oil and vinegar into the kale with your hands for about 1 minute, until the liquid is evenly dispersed and the texture of the kale is softer. Divide the mixture into 2 smaller bowls and set an avocado half on top of each bed of kale.

In the same bowl the kale was massaged in, add the quinoa, hummus, bell pepper, cucumber, tomato, onion, lemon juice, salt, and pepper. Mix with a spoon until well combined.

Divide the mixture atop the avocados, filling the middle and overflowing into the bowl of kale. Sprinkle with smoked paprika and pepitas (if using).

YIELD 2 bowls

TIP

To half the avocado, slice through the avocado with a large knife lengthwise until you feel the knife hit the pit. Then rotate the avocado on the knife to make a cut around the pit. Twist the two halves apart. To remove the seed, aim the sharp edge of the knife blade at the pit and whack it hard enough so it sticks in the pit, then twist the knife to pull out the pit. To remove the skin, slip a spoon between the avocado and the skin. Carefully run the spoon along the edge, loosening the avocado from its skin.

GARLICKY NOOCH BROCCOLI AND POTATOES

NOOCH! The affectionate nickname for the beloved ingredient nutritional yeast that the world is coming to love. Nutritional yeast is finding its way onto mainstream supermarket shelves because of its nutty and cheesy flavors. Some find it's the perfect replacement for Parmesan cheese. In my last two books, I use it combined with walnuts and hemp seeds to make a parmesan, but I also love it on its own. Nutritional yeast is the perfect finishing touch to this sheet pan packed with everyone's favorite combination of potatoes and broccoli.

+ 1½ pounds (about 5 cups [680 g]) petite potatoes, halved
+ 3 tablespoons (45 ml) olive oil, divided
+ 1 head of broccoli, cut into bite-size pieces
+ 4 cloves garlic, minced
+ 1 tablespoon (15 g) Italian seasoning
+ ½ teaspoon sea salt
+ ¼ teaspoon black pepper
+ ¼ cup (20 g) nutritional yeast
+ 2 tablespoons (8 g) chopped fresh parsley

Preheat the oven to 425°F (220°C, or gas mark 7). Line a sheet pan with parchment paper.

Add the potatoes to the sheet pan and drizzle with 1 tablespoon (15 ml) olive oil. Place in the oven and bake for 20 minutes.

Remove from the oven. Add the broccoli and drizzle with the remaining olive oil. Add the garlic, Italian seasoning, salt, and pepper, and toss until well combined. Return the sheet pan to the oven and bake for 10 minutes, until the tips of the florets have started to brown and the potatoes are fork-tender.

Remove from the oven, sprinkle with nutritional yeast and parsley, and toss to combine. Serve as a side dish or atop a big bowl of massaged kale (page 27) for a complete meal.

YIELD 6 servings

TIP
Add this to a bowl with baked tofu, quinoa, chickpeas, and some greens for a complete, protein-packed meal.

NOT-SO-TUNA JACKFRUIT MACARONI SALAD OR MELT

The traditional flavors of tuna salad you love made with easily accessible jackfruit from a can. The crunch of veggies and pungent pops of flavor from the mustard and relish make this a recipe to return to again and again. I can't get enough! I also love doubling this salad and taking it to picnics or portioning it out into containers for a road trip. It hits the spot every time. The tuna melts pair perfectly with a pickle and side of potato chips!

FOR NOT-SO-TUNA JACKFRUIT:

+ 1½ cups (353 g) canned jackfruit, drained, squeezed dry, and shredded
+ 1 celery stalk, minced
+ 2 tablespoons (20 g) minced red onion
+ 1 tablespoon (4 g) roughly chopped fresh parsley
+ 1 tablespoon (15 g) sweet pickle relish
+ 3 tablespoons (45 g) vegan mayonnaise
+ 2 teaspoons (10 g) Dijon mustard
+ ¼ teaspoon sea salt, plus more to taste
+ Pinch black pepper, plus more to taste

FOR MACARONI SALAD:

+ 1 cup (235 g) macaroni, uncooked
+ 1 cup (150 g) frozen peas
+ ¼ cup (60 g) vegan mayonnaise
+ Smoked paprika (optional)

FOR MELT:

+ 4 slices thick vegan bread
+ Vegan butter
+ 2 slices vegan cheese of choice (American or cheddar recommended)
+ 2 teaspoons (10 ml) water

To make the not-so-tuna jackfruit:
Add the jackfruit, celery, onion, parsley, relish, mayonnaise, Dijon mustard, salt, and pepper to a bowl. Mix until well combined. Add more salt and pepper to taste. Serve atop greens or follow the steps to make macaroni salad or tuna melt.

To make macaroni salad:
Prepare the pasta according to package directions. Add the peas in the final minute of boiling, then drain the pasta and peas. Combine the pasta, prepared Not-So-Tuna Jackfruit, and mayonnaise, and mix until well combined. Cover and chill in the refrigerator for 30 minutes, or until chilled completely. Serve sprinkled with smoked paprika (if using).

To make tuna melts:
Spread butter on 1 side of each slice of bread. Heat a large skillet over medium heat and have the lid on standby. Add 1 slice of bread to the skillet, buttered-side down, then top with half of the Not-So-Tuna Jackfruit mixture and 1 slice of vegan cheese. Let the bread toast for about 1 minute, then add 1 teaspoon of water and quickly put the lid on to trap the steam into the skillet. Leave covered for 40 to 60 seconds, allowing the cheese to fully melt. Remove the lid and top with another piece of buttered bread, buttered-side up. Carefully flip the sandwich and grill for 2 to 4 minutes, until both sides are browned. Repeat for the second sandwich.

YIELD 2 cups Not-So-Tuna Jackfruit / 4 cups macaroni salad / 2 Not-So-Tuna Jackfruit Melts

TIP
The Not-So-Tuna Jackfruit Salad will keep for up to 7 days in the refrigerator, making it perfect for meal prep!

DUSTIN'S FAVORITE SUMMER SALAD

This is a dream to take to a summer cookout. Its fresh ingredients are vibrant in color and flavor and very inviting when sitting on a table typically filled with chips, macaroni salad, and hot dogs. This was a staple of mine way before I even considered going vegan. To avoid the avocado getting brown, cut it fresh and add it to the salad once you get to the party.

+ 1 pint (474 g) cherry tomatoes, halved

+ 2 cups (328 g) fresh corn (or frozen, thawed to room temperature)

+ 2 avocados, peeled and diced

+ ¼ cup (10 g) fresh basil, roughly chopped

+ 1 tablespoon (15 ml) olive oil

+ Juice of 1 lime

+ ½ teaspoon sea salt, or more to taste

+ ½ teaspoon black pepper, or more to taste

+ 2 scallions, thinly sliced

Add the tomatoes, corn, avocado, basil, olive oil, lime juice, salt, and black pepper to a large bowl. Mix until well combined. Sprinkle with additional salt and pepper, if desired. Top with scallions. Serve family style.

YIELD 6 to 8 servings

TIP

When I have time, I like to sauté the corn in a dash of oil, salt, and pepper in a hot skillet just until lightly browned to get a rustic look. Then I let it cool and mix it with everything else. It's really a matter of preference. The fresh crunch of the corn uncooked is a delightful texture to pair with the creamy avocado, too!

SKILLET-KISSED GREEN BEANS AND RED GRAPES

I once had a variation of this dish at a housewarming party and haven't been able to forget it! I have since made this for several clients, always to rave reviews, and it's also a favorite in our home. The balance of earthiness from the green beans with the richness of the olive oil and the touch of juicy tartness from the grapes makes this a unique dish. Hopefully it finds a spot in your regular menu rotation as well.

+ 2 tablespoons (30 ml) olive oil, divided
+ ½ red onion, thinly sliced
+ 4 garlic cloves, minced
+ 4 cups (12 ounces/360 g) green beans, trimmed and cut into 2-inch (5-cm) pieces
+ 1½ cups (260 g) seedless red grapes, halved
+ ½ teaspoon sea salt, plus more to taste
+ Black pepper (optional)
+ Slivered almonds (optional)

Heat 1 tablespoon (15 ml) of oil in a large skillet over medium heat. Add the onion and sauté for 3 minutes, until soft. Add the garlic and sauté for 1 minute, until fragrant.

Add the remaining oil to the skillet. Add the green beans and grapes and cook for 6 to 8 minutes, tossing occasionally, until everything is heated through and the grapes have begun to wilt slightly. Add the salt and toss until well combined.

Season to taste. Transfer to a serving platter and sprinkle with slivered almonds (if using).

YIELD 4 servings

TIP

You can buy prepared green beans in a 12-ounce (340 g) bag. I used this amount to make it as easy as possible if you go this route. You can also use frozen if you wish. Just follow the same instructions and be sure the beans get cooked all the way through in the allotted cooking time.

WARM ROTINI AND SPINACH PESTO PASTA SALAD

I love sneaking my greens in any way that I can, and what better way than tossing them with tasty carbs and this robust pesto sauce. This is a simple recipe to pull together on a Sunday afternoon when I'm working around the house or when guests pop over for an unannounced visit. I also love it as a meal prep option. It's a nice comfort food to enjoy on hump day to get you through the midweek slump!

+ 2 cups (195 g) rotini pasta or gluten-free pasta of choice
+ 2 cups (60 g) baby spinach
+ 1 cup (150 g) cherry tomatoes, halved
+ 1 batch Presto Pesto (page 50)
+ Crushed red pepper (optional)

Cook the pasta according to package directions. Drain the pasta, and add the spinach and cherry tomatoes to the pot. Add the hot pasta back to the pot and top with pesto. Mix everything until well combined and the spinach has just slightly wilted. The spinach will still hold its shape some, but it will be softer and more malleable.

Serve warm sprinkled with crushed red pepper (if using).

YIELD 4 servings

TIP

While this is meant to be served warm, you can absolutely portion it into meal prep containers and eat it cold. You can also reheat it in the microwave or on the stove top up to 3 days after making it. The green pesto will get darker in color when eaten as a leftover, but it's still edible and delicious.

FIESTA QUINOA BOWL WITH SWEET LIME VINAIGRETTE

This is not your average taco salad, but it's full of the robust flavors we know and love in a traditional taco bowl. This version is very grain-and-veggie forward with an abundance of greens. The irresistible sweet vinaigrette with spiced quinoa will satiate anyone's appetite. Pro tip on this simple and delicious vinaigrette is to double or triple the recipe to have some on hand in the refrigerator. It will last up to three weeks in an airtight container.

FOR SWEET LIME VINAIGRETTE:

+ ⅓ cup (80 ml) olive oil
+ Juice of 1½ limes
+ 2 tablespoons (28 ml) agave
+ ¼ teaspoon sea salt

FOR FIESTA QUINOA BOWL:

+ 3 cups (555 g) Quick Quinoa (page 20) or cooked quinoa
+ 2 teaspoons (4 g) chili powder
+ 2 cups (134 g) kale, stems removed and roughly chopped into small pieces
+ 1 can (15 ounces/425 g) black beans, drained and rinsed
+ 1 red bell pepper, seeded and diced
+ 1 cup (164 g) frozen or fresh corn, thawed if frozen
+ Sea salt
+ 2 avocados, peeled and sliced

+ Instant Almond Cheese Crumble (page 33, optional)
+ 1 bunch scallions, thinly sliced (optional)
+ Pepitas (optional)
+ Chopped fresh cilantro (optional)

To make the sweet lime vinaigrette:
Combine the oil, lime juice, agave, and salt in a bowl or container with an airtight lid or salad dressing shaker. Mix or shake with the sealed lid tightly on until well combined. Set aside.

To make the fiesta quinoa bowl:
Combine the quinoa and chili powder in a bowl. Add the kale, black beans, bell pepper, and corn to the bowl, and mix until well combined. Add the lime vinaigrette to taste, and toss until well combined. Add salt to taste.

Serve in one big bowl family-style with avocados fanned out on top or portion into meal prep containers for quick and easy meals throughout the week. If meal prepping, add the avocado fresh when consuming.

Garnish with Instant Almond Cheese Crumble, scallions, pepitas, and cilantro (if using).

YIELD 6 servings

> **TIP**
> Quinoa is available premade now if you are short on time, either in the same section as instant rice or the frozen section of the grocery store. Or follow the steps for Quick Quinoa (page 20). Of course, you can replace the canned black beans with 1¾ cups (292 g) black beans from the Basic Betty Beans recipe (page 21) if you prefer.

THE BEET GOES ON SHEET-PAN BOWL

The beet is an underutilized vegetable, and I get it: It's messy to cut, getting red juices everywhere. This bowl offers up a quick and easy way to build a bountiful bowl that is vibrant with color and bursting with flavor. This is one of those easy one-sheet-pan meals that makes prep an easy, no-fuss situation with flavorful results.

FOR EASY TAHINI DRESSING:

+ ¼ cup (60 g) tahini
+ Juice of ½ lemon
+ 1 tablespoon (20 g) maple syrup
+ ¼ teaspoon sea salt
+ Water, as needed

FOR SHEET-PAN BOWL:

+ 1 large beet, peeled and cut into ½-inch (1-cm) chunks
+ 1 medium sweet potato, cut into ½-inch (1-cm) chunks
+ 1 can (15 ounces/425 g) chickpeas, drained and rinsed
+ Cooking spray
+ ½ teaspoon ground turmeric
+ ½ teaspoon sea salt
+ ¼ teaspoon black pepper
+ 4 cups (115 g) massaged kale (page 27)
+ 1 cup (185 g) Quick Quinoa (page 20)
+ Avocado, peeled and sliced
+ Hemp seeds (optional)

Preheat the oven to 425°F (220°C, or gas mark 7). Line a sheet pan with parchment paper.

To make the tahini dressing:
Add the tahini, lemon juice, maple syrup, and salt to a bowl. Whisk until smooth and creamy. Add 1 teaspoon of water as needed to reach desired dressing consistency.

To make the sheet-pan bowls:
Create a separate row of beets, sweet potato, and chickpeas on the sheet pan. Spray everything with cooking spray, and sprinkle with salt and pepper. Sprinkle just the chickpeas with turmeric. Toss each vegetable separately to combine with seasoning.

Bake for 15 minutes, flip everything with a spatula, and mix everything to combine. Bake for 15 minutes, or until the sweet potatoes are fork-tender. Remove everything from the oven and allow to cool.

Build 4 bowls, each with 1 cup (28 g) of kale, ¼ cup (46 g) of quinoa, and one-quarter of the avocado. Divide the contents of the sheet pan evenly among the 4 bowls. Drizzle the dressing evenly among the 4 bowls. Sprinkle with hemp seeds (if using).

YIELD 4 bowls

TIP

If making ahead for meal prep, leave off the avocado. Rub cut leftover avocado with lime or lemon juice and store with the avocado pit intact wrapped tightly to help avoid oxidizing. Use leftover or unused avocado within the next 2 days as needed. While the prep for this meal is easy, it can get messy! If you prefer, swap out red beets with golden beets to avoid a red beet juice mess. Golden beets are slightly sweeter, but they hold the same nutritional value and require the same cooking time as red beets.

LEMON AND GARLIC AND THYME, OH MY!

Lemon and garlic, combined with the earthiness of thyme, and mixed into a hearty brown rice is super tasty and very satisfying. If I have cooked rice on hand that needs to get used up, I turn to this recipe. It's simple and I always have the ingredients in my pantry. It's also a perfect dish to make for meal prep.

+ 1 tablespoon (15 ml) olive oil
+ 1 onion, chopped
+ 3 cloves garlic, minced
+ ½ teaspoon dried thyme
+ ½ teaspoon sea salt
+ 2 cups Rice Realness (page 20) or Cauliflower Rice for the Win (page 32)
+ Juice of ½ lemon
+ 4 cups (115 g) massaged kale (page 27)

Heat the olive oil in a medium skillet over medium heat. Add the onion and sauté for 3 minutes, until the onions are soft. Add the garlic, thyme, and salt. Sauté for 1 minute, until fragrant. Remove from the heat, and add the rice and lemon juice. Mix until well combined.

Divide the massaged kale between 2 bowls and top each with the rice mixture. Serve warm.

YIELD 2 bowls

TIP

This is a fun one to build on. I love adding Basic Betty Beans (page 21), baked tempeh (page 25), or baked tofu (page 34), for a complete meal. Or sometimes I split it into 4 portions and use it as a side in a smaller compartment of my meal prep container.

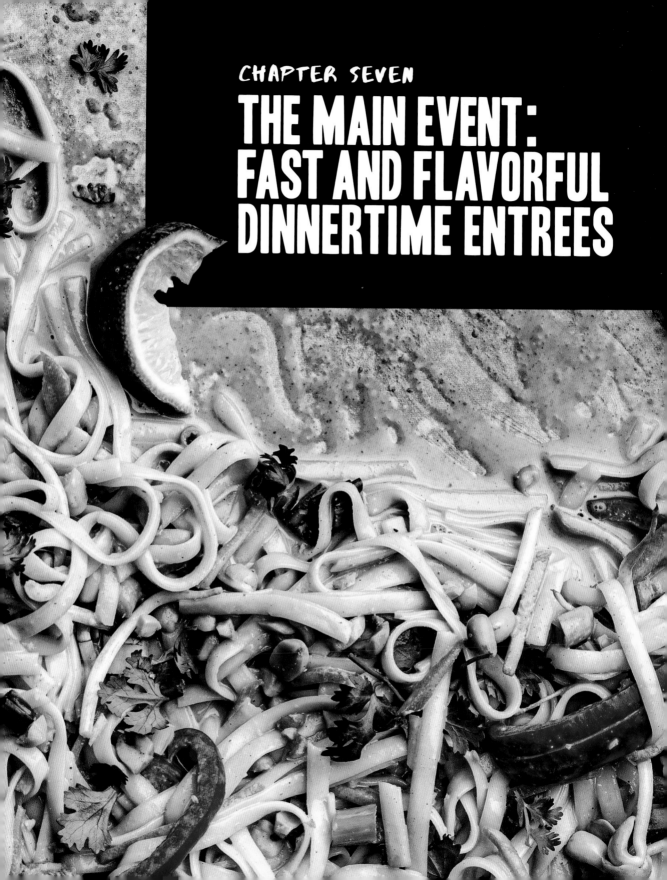

CHAPTER SEVEN

THE MAIN EVENT: FAST AND FLAVORFUL DINNERTIME ENTREES

CREAMY SPINACH AND ARTICHOKE LASAGNA

Spinach and artichoke dip is a party favorite (see tip) because of its irresistible creamy texture with satisfying spinach and chunks of artichoke hearts. In this entree version of the party favorite, I put it all together in several decadent layers for a carb lover's paradise. Take it a step further and serve with a side of Miso-Garlic Cheese Bread (page 79). It's worth mentioning, some people soak their noodles: DO NOT SOAK the noodles for this recipe. It was created without soaking noodles, and the amount of sauce is perfect to hydrate the no-bake noodles for an al dente finish.

+ Cooking spray
+ 1 can (14 ounces/396 g) artichoke hearts, roughly chopped
+ 1 package (10 ounces/280 g) frozen chopped spinach, thawed and squeezed dry
+ 1 block (14 ounces/396 g) extra-firm tofu, drained and crumbled
+ 1 teaspoon garlic powder
+ 1 teaspoon onion powder
+ 1 teaspoon sea salt
+ 1 batch Alfredo sauce (page 150)
+ 8 no-cook lasagna noodles
+ 1⅓ cups (153 g) vegan mozzarella shreds
+ Italian seasoning (optional)
+ Crushed red pepper (optional)

Preheat the oven to 375°F (190°C, or gas mark 5). Grease an 8 x 8–inch (20 x 20–cm) baking dish with cooking spray.

In a bowl, combine the artichoke hearts, spinach, tofu, garlic powder, onion powder, and salt. Mix until well combined, being sure to break up the spinach so it is evenly dispersed.

To build the lasagna, spread ½ cup (120 ml) of the Alfredo sauce on the bottom of the greased 8 x 8–inch (20 x 20–cm) baking dish.

Add 2 noodles side by side and top with 1⅓ cups (269 g) tofu filling topped with ¾ cup (175 ml) Alfredo sauce and finished with ⅓ cup (38 g) mozzarella cheese. Repeat this step two more times with the same measurements, creating 3 layers of filling total. Top with the final 2 noodles, remaining Alfredo sauce, and remaining mozzarella shreds. Sprinkle lightly with Italian seasoning and crushed red pepper (if using).

The lasagna should come right to the top of the baking dish. Place a piece of parchment paper over the lasagna and place an inverted sheet pan or aluminum foil over the baking dish. The sheet pan should be big enough that the baking dish fits under the edges of the sheet pan.

Bake for 25 minutes, remove the sheet pan, and gently peel back the parchment. Bake for 10 minutes, uncovered, until the cheese has melted and the sides have started to bubble. Remove from the oven and let sit for 15 minutes. Cut into 6 slices.

YIELD 6 servings

TIPS

If you can't find no-cook noodles, just cook traditional lasagna noodles as directed and use kitchen shears to cut an inch or two off the end to fit the pan as you are layering the lasagna.

To create an epic spinach artichoke dip appetizer, combine the tofu mixture from this lasagna with the Alfredo sauce and bake at 375°F (190°C, or gas mark 5) for 35 minutes or until heated through and the top is golden brown. Serve with tortilla chips or pita.

STOVE TOP MUSHROOM TETRAZZINI

My mother used to make a really tasty chicken tetrazzini bake when I was a kid, and I have been wanting to make one for some time. I love the robust flavors paired with the joy and comfort pasta inevitably brings to the table. And this stove top version comes together so quickly. With everything being cooked in one pot, you don't even have to drain the pasta. And hey, a little fun fact, tetrazzini is actually named after the Italian opera star Luisa Tetrazzini. I thank Lady Tetrazzini for this abundant dish of Italian goodness!

+ ¼ cup (55 g) vegan butter
+ 1 onion, diced
+ 16 ounces (454 g) sliced baby bella or cremini mushrooms
+ 6 cloves garlic
+ 2 tablespoons (28 ml) white wine vinegar
+ 4 cups (940 ml) vegetable broth or Scrappy Veggie Broth (page 35)
+ 1 pound (454 g) spaghetti
+ 1½ cups (225 g) frozen peas
+ ½ cup (40 g) nutritional yeast
+ ¼ cup (30 g) bread crumbs or gluten-free bread crumbs
+ 1½ teaspoons sea salt
+ ½ teaspoon black pepper
+ 1 tablespoon (15 g) Italian seasoning
+ ¼ cup (15 g) chopped fresh parsley
+ Crushed red pepper (optional)

Melt the butter in a stockpot over medium heat. Add the onion and mushrooms. Sauté for 4 to 6 minutes, until the mushrooms have reduced in size. Add the garlic and sauté for 1 minute, until fragrant. Add the white wine vinegar and sauté for 2 to 4 minutes, until the vinegar evaporates.

Add the vegetable broth and bring to a boil. Add the spaghetti, breaking it if need be so it fits in the pan submerged by the broth. Continue to boil and cook the pasta according to the package directions, stirring occasionally to keep the noodles from sticking and moving them around to cook evenly. Add the peas to the pot in the final 2 minutes of cooking. Do not drain the pasta.

When the pasta is cooked to your liking (al dente suggested), add the nutritional yeast, breadcrumbs, salt, pepper, Italian seasoning, and parsley. Toss until everything is well combined and the pasta is evenly coated. Divide into serving bowls and garnish with freshly cracked pepper (if using).

YIELD 8 servings

TIP

Use 1 pound (454 g) of your favorite type of pasta in place of the spaghetti if you wish! Using a smaller pasta makes it easier to mix up the ingredients. Traditionally tetrazzini is made with a long pasta, and I also prefer spaghetti, but I encourage you to pick your favorite or use whatever type you have on hand.

ONE-POT POMODORO PUTTANESCA

Sauce and pasta is always a home run. Dish up Mediterranean flavors of kalamata olives and capers to make your dinner guest feel like they are getting treated to a unique, high-end pasta experience. Use the Instant Almond Cheese Crumble (page 33) as a parmesan cheese to take it all the way. If you are cutting back on oil, simply sauté your veggies in vegetable broth and forget the drizzle of oil on the final plated serving.

+ 2 tablespoons (30 ml) olive oil, plus extra for drizzling
+ 1 onion, roughly chopped
+ 6 cloves garlic, roughly chopped
+ 1 pint (474 g) cherry tomatoes, whole
+ 3 cups (720 ml) vegetable broth or Scrappy Veggie Broth (page 35)
+ 2 (28 ounces/793 g) cans crushed tomatoes
+ 1 pound (454 g) linguine or spaghetti
+ 1 cup (128 g) pitted kalamata olives, roughly chopped
+ 2 tablespoons (17 g) capers, drained
+ ¼ cup (15 g) chopped fresh parsley, plus more for garnish
+ 1 teaspoon sea salt
+ ½ teaspoon black pepper
+ Instant Almond Cheese Crumble (page 33, optional)
+ Crushed red pepper (optional)

Heat the oil in a large stockpot or skillet with a lid. Add the onion and sauté for 3 minutes, until soft. Add the garlic and sauté for 1 minute, until fragrant. Add the cherry tomatoes, vegetable broth, and tomatoes. Stir to combine, cover, and bring to a boil.

Break the pasta in half and submerge in the liquid. Place the lid on the pot and cook for 12 to 14 minutes, or until al dente according to package directions, stirring frequently. If the pasta is not cooked after 14 minutes, place the lid on and continue to cook, stirring and checking every 2 minutes for desired doneness.

Remove from the heat. Add the olives, capers, parsley, salt, and pepper to the pasta, and mix to combine. Serve warm, drizzled with olive oil, and sprinkled with parsley, Instant Almond Cheese Crumble, and crushed red pepper (if using).

YIELD 6 to 8 servings

TIP

Puttanesca ingredients typically include tomatoes, olive oil, anchovies, olives, capers, and garlic, in addition to pasta. Play with your food and mix it up! Add ingredients into this that you love and enjoy. If capers and olives aren't your thing, go bananas and add things that make your personal taste buds sing.

BAKED NOT SO STIR-FRY IN A FLASH

I always get impatient when frying tofu, but I found I could skip all that by adding all of my favorite stir-fry goodies to a sheet pan, baking it in the oven, and setting my table for dinner while it cooks! The muss and fuss of standing over the stove monitoring my tofu is gone from the equation in this version bursting with fresh vegetables, Chinese spice, and succulent tofu.

+ ½ red onion, cut into chunks
+ 1 red bell pepper, roughly chopped
+ ½ head broccoli, stems removed, cut into bite-size florets
+ 8 ounces (225 g) baby bella mushrooms, stemmed and sliced
+ 1 block (14 ounces/396 g) extra-firm tofu, cut into ½-inch (1-cm) cubes
+ 2 tablespoons (30 ml) sesame oil
+ 3 tablespoons (45 ml) soy sauce
+ 1 teaspoon, Chinese five-spice powder (optional)
+ ½ teaspoon sea salt
+ ½ teaspoon garlic powder
+ Rice Realness, Cauliflower Rice for the Win, or Quick Quinoa (page 20 or page 32, optional)

Preheat the oven to 425°F (220°C, or gas mark 7). Line a sheet pan with parchment paper.

In a large bowl, combine the onion, bell pepper, broccoli, mushrooms, and tofu. Drizzle with sesame oil and soy sauce, and gently toss until everything is coated. Add the Chinese five-spice powder (if using), salt, and garlic powder, and gently toss to coat.

Transfer to the prepared sheet pan and spread in one layer. Bake for 15 minutes, flip everything, and bake for 15 minutes, until the tofu has started to lightly crisp up and broccoli has started to char.

Serve with rice, cauliflower rice, or quinoa for a complete dish.

YIELD 6 servings

TIP

Traditionally used in Chinese cuisine, Chinese five-spice powder is a great spice to have on hand. I like to use it as a rub for tofu, seitan, and tempeh. I want to stress that if you don't have it and don't plan on buying it, that's okay! Simply omit it from this recipe and it will still be tasty.

TOASTY PEAR, WALNUT, AND ARUGULA FLATBREAD

Naan is a perfect option for a quick flatbread, but sometimes a vegan naan can be hard to find. A thin-crust pizza dough will work just fine or even a tortilla in a pinch (see tip). The subtle, juicy, fruit-forward sweetness of the pears with the creamy hummus and zippy dash of balsamic make this flatbread an impressive quick dinner to serve friends at wine-o-clock!

+ 12 oz (340 g) store-bought vegan thin-crust pizza dough or pizza dough
+ 2 tablespoons (30 ml) olive oil, divided
+ 1 package (10 ounces/280 g) store-bought hummus
+ 1 cup (235 g) pear, cored and thinly sliced
+ ½ cup (58 g) red onion, thinly sliced
+ ½ cup (60 g) walnuts, chopped
+ ½ cup (57 g) vegan mozzarella shreds
+ 1 cup (20 g) baby arugula
+ 2 pinches teaspoon sea salt
+ 2 tablespoons (28 ml) balsamic glaze

Preheat the oven to 425°F (220°C, or gas mark 7). Line a large sheet pan with parchment paper.

Roll or stretch the pizza dough to fit the sheet pan. Brush the dough with 1 tablespoon plus 2 teaspoons (25 ml) olive oil. Place the sheet pan in the oven and bake for 4 minutes.

Remove from the oven and spread the hummus in one layer over the dough. Add pear slices, onion, and walnuts, and sprinkle with mozzarella until evenly covered. Return to the oven and bake for 12 to 14 minutes, until the cheese is melted and edges of flatbread have browned.

While flatbread is baking, add the arugula and remaining olive oil to a bowl with salt. Toss until arugula is evenly coated.

Remove the pizza from the oven. Top with the dressed arugula, and drizzle with balsamic glaze.

YIELD 12 pieces

TIP

If you are struggling to find vegan naan or pizza dough, use two burrito-size tortillas to make your flatbread. Since the tortillas are so thin, only brush each tortilla with 1 teaspoon of olive oil and prebake for just 3 minutes before adding toppings to avoid burning.

WHOLE ROASTED MAPLE-DIJON CAULIFLOWER

I first enjoyed a whole roasted cauliflower at ABC Kitchen in New York City with my dear friend Ashley Madden, who also happens to be the brilliant photographer for this book and the previous *Epic Vegan* book. I was so blown away by the versatility of this vegetable that I had to come up with a version of my very own using pantry staples I love: maple syrup and Dijon. I recommend going the extra mile and serve it with the Easy Tahini Dressing (page 136), but if you don't, it's still super easy and very satisfying! The only clincher here is that it takes an hour to roast, but I promise you it's worth the wait.

+ 3 tablespoons (45 ml) olive oil, divided

+ Juice of ½ lemon

+ 2 tablespoons (10 g) nutritional yeast

+ 2 tablespoons (30 g) Dijon mustard

+ 2 teaspoons (14 g) maple syrup

+ ¾ teaspoon sea salt

+ 1 head cauliflower

+ Easy Tahini Dressing (page 136, optional)

+ 1 teaspoon chopped fresh parsley

+ Smoked paprika (optional)

Preheat the oven to 425°F (220°C, or gas mark 7).

In a small bowl, combine 2 tablespoons (30 ml) of the olive oil, lemon juice, nutritional yeast, Dijon mustard, maple syrup, and salt.

Remove the leaves, stem, and core from the head of cauliflower so it sets flat. Be careful to leave the head intact.

Set the cauliflower with the floret-side down in an 8 x 8-inch (20 x 20–cm) baking dish and drizzle the remaining olive oil inside the crevices of the cauliflower. Flip the cauliflower on its base with the florets facing upward and use a pastry brush to coat the cauliflower with the maple mixture. See the recipe tip if you don't have a pastry brush.

Use aluminum foil to cover the cauliflower and seal the edges to trap steam. Bake for 1 hour.

Remove from the oven and let sit for 10 minutes. Transfer to a serving platter. Drizzle with Easy Tahini Dressing (if using), then sprinkle with parsley. Sprinkle a dash of smoked paprika (if using) for a little extra color pop when serving.

Cut into 4 wedges to serve.

YIELD 4 servings

TIP

If you don't have a pastry brush, a paper towel or coffee filter makes a great substitute in a pinch. Simply dip the corner of the towel or filter in the miso mixture and then brush the mixture on the food as directed. If you own a Dutch oven, I recommend it in this recipe as an alternative to using a baking dish with aluminum foil.

BOW-TIE ALFREDO WITH BROCCOLI AND SUN-DRIED TOMATOES

When I think of Alfredo, I think of creamy decadence and this sauce offers up just that! I like bow-tie (farfalle) pasta because of its fun shape and it's easy to fork. If you prefer your Alfredo with fettuccine, I certainly won't stop you! Add vegan chicken atop this dish for a nostalgic twist.

FOR ALFREDO SAUCE:

+ 1½ cups (205 g) raw cashews, soaked overnight or boiled for 10 minutes and drained
+ 2 cups (475 ml) water
+ 1 teaspoon garlic powder
+ 1 teaspoon onion powder
+ 2 teaspoons (10 g) sea salt
+ Juice of ½ lemon
+ 3 tablespoons (15 g) nutritional yeast
+ ½ teaspoon dried rosemary
+ ¾ teaspoon black pepper

FOR PASTA:

+ 1 pound (454 g) bow-tie pasta
+ 1 head broccoli, cut into bite-size florets
+ 1 cup (55 g) sun-dried tomatoes, roughly chopped

To make the Alfredo sauce:
Combine the cashews, water, garlic powder, onion powder, salt, lemon juice, nutritional yeast, rosemary, and pepper in a blender. Blend for 1 to 2 minutes, until smooth and creamy.

To make the pasta:
Cook the pasta according to package directions. During the last 2 minutes of cooking, add the broccoli and sun-dried tomatoes to the boiling water. Cook until the desired doneness of pasta is reached (al dente is recommended).

Drain the pasta and vegetables, and then return them to the pot they were cooked in. Add the sauce to the pasta and vegetables, and mix until everything is coated. Serve warm.

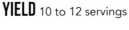

YIELD 10 to 12 servings

TIP

The Alfredo sauce can be made ahead of time and kept in an airtight container in the refrigerator for up to 1 week. It's great to have on hand to mix with freshly cooked pasta for a quick dinner or lunch.

ONE-PAN SUPER SAUCY GARLIC ZITI

Pasta and sauce would be my meal of choice—all day, every day—if I had it my way! I love this simple quick roast of garlic to add a punch of garlicky goodness to this traditional saucy dish. The main issue I always have with ziti is that it isn't saucy enough because the pasta soaks up the sauce when it bakes. I took care of that here, upping the sauce game, so you get those robust sauce flavors and your carbs with every spoonful.

+ 12 cloves garlic, halved
+ ½ onion, roughly chopped
+ ¼ cup (59 ml) olive oil
+ 1 pound (454 g) ziti or penne pasta, cooked
+ 2 cups (228 g) vegan mozzarella shreds, divided
+ ½ teaspoon sea salt
+ ¼ teaspoon crushed red pepper, plus more for sprinkling
+ ¼ teaspoon black pepper
+ 2 jars (24 ounces/682 ml) marinara
+ Italian seasoning (optional)

Preheat the oven to 375°F (190°C, or gas mark 5).

Add the garlic, onions, and olive oil to a 9 x 13–inch (23 x 33–cm) baking dish. Bake for 16 minutes, until the garlic has started to brown slightly and the onions have slightly reduced in size.

Remove the baking dish from the oven. Add the cooked pasta, 1½ cups (171 g) mozzarella shreds, salt, crushed red pepper, pepper, and marinara to the baking dish. Mix everything until well combined. Top with remaining mozzarella, Italian seasoning (if using), and more crushed red pepper if desired.

Bake for 30 minutes, until the cheese has melted and edges are bubbling.

YIELD 8 to 10 servings

TIP

If you aren't a fan of store-bought mozzarella shreds, use the 3-Minute Cashew Cream Sauce (page 33) in place of the shreds. Divide it up exactly as stated in this recipe. Instead of sprinkling the remaining half cup, drizzle it over the top. If you prep ahead, you can also freeze the cream sauce and grate it on a cheese grater for shreds. Feel free to get deluxe with a meatball ziti by preparing one package of store-bought vegan meatballs and slicing them in half. Mix them into the pasta with everything else and then bake as directed.

CHEESESTEAK STUFFED PEPPERS

In *Epic Vegan*, I went to great lengths to offer up what I consider to be a truly fantastic Philly Cheesesteak Sandwich. In this book, I ditched the bread factor and house the goods in one of the main cheesesteak elements, the green pepper. The pepper is vibrant and fresh and adds a delicious new take on this nostalgic classic. This is also a super fun one for dinner dates as it's a nice little conversation starter, with it being a twist on an old standby.

+ 1 onion, sliced
+ 8 ounces (225 g) cremini or baby bella mushrooms, sliced
+ 1 cup (235 g) seitan, thinly sliced
+ 2 tablespoons (30 ml) olive oil
+ ½ teaspoon sea salt
+ ¼ teaspoon black pepper
+ 2 tablespoons (28 ml) soy sauce
+ 2 large green bell peppers
+ 1 cup (115 g) vegan cheddar shreds or Punk Cheddah sauce (page 157)
+ 2 scallions, thinly sliced

Preheat the oven to 425°F (220°C, or gas mark 7). Line a sheet pan with parchment paper.

Add the onion, mushrooms, and seitan to the sheet pan. Drizzle with oil, sprinkle with salt and pepper, and toss to combine. Add the soy sauce, and toss one more time to coat the ingredients. Bake for 15 minutes.

While that is baking, cut the bell peppers in half lengthwise. Remove the stem, core, and seeds. (You can save these for a batch of Scrappy Veggie Broth, page 35). Add 2 tablespoons (14 g) of cheese to the inside of each pepper.

Remove the sheet pan from the oven. Divide the mixture among the 4 pepper halves. Top with remaining cheese and bake the stuffed peppers for 35 minutes, until the skin on the peppers is just starting to shrivel and the cheese has melted.

Top with scallions.

YIELD 2 servings

TIP

As vegan cheeses go, they have come a long way but they still are not the same as traditional dairy cheeses. If you can't find vegan cheddar shreds, use mozzarella or whatever you can find. If you prefer provolone, which is often used on a typical cheesesteak sandwich, there is a brand of vegan provolone slices. Cut them up and use in place of the shreds. It's not that serious. Swap out vegan cheese variations as needed for the same ooey gooey cheesesteak results!

COCO LOCO PAD THAI

Creamy, luscious, and decadent is what I think of when I think of coconut. Paired with the divine peanut, it's the sauce of all sauces. Drizzle it on veggies, toss baked tofu in it, or dip Baked Thai Chili Cauliflower Bites (page 70) in it! You can always stay on the healthy side and use it with spiralized noodles (page 24). It really is a great sauce to have on hand to take your meal prep to the next level.

FOR COCO LOCO PEANUT SAUCE:

+ ¾ cup (175 ml) canned coconut milk
+ ¼ cup (80 g) maple syrup
+ 2 tablespoons (28 ml) soy sauce or gluten-free tamari
+ Juice of ½ lime
+ 1 tablespoon (15 ml) seasoned rice vinegar
+ 1 tablespoon (15 ml) toasted sesame oil
+ ½ cup (130 g) creamy peanut butter
+ 1 tablespoon (15 ml) chili garlic sauce
+ ½ teaspoon ginger powder
+ ½ teaspoon garlic powder
+ ¼ teaspoon sea salt

FOR PAD THAI:

+ 1 box (14 ounces/396 g) thin rice noodles
+ 2 tablespoons (30 ml) toasted sesame oil, divided
+ 1 red bell pepper, thinly sliced
+ 1 cup (235 g) shredded or matchstick carrot
+ 1 bunch scallions, cut into 2-inch (5-cm) strips
+ Canned or fresh bean sprouts, drained
+ Crushed peanuts (optional)
+ Lime wedges (optional)
+ Chopped fresh cilantro (optional)

To make the coco loco peanut sauce:

Shake the can of coconut up to make sure the liquid and fat mix together well. Add the ¾ cup (175 ml) of coconut milk, maple syrup, soy sauce, lime juice, vinegar, oil, peanut butter, chili garlic sauce, ginger powder, garlic powder, and salt to a blender. Blend until smooth and creamy.

To make the pad thai:

Cook the noodles according to package directions, drain, and toss with 1 tablespoon (15 ml) of sesame oil. In the same pot the noodles were cooked in, heat the remaining sesame oil. Add the bell pepper and carrot. Sauté for 2 to 4 minutes, until starting to soften. Add the scallions and cook for 1 minute, until soft. Add the pasta and peanut sauce, and toss until combined. Divide among 6 bowls and garnish with sprouts, crushed peanuts, and cilantro (if using). Serve warm.

YIELD 6 servings pad thai and 2 cups (475 ml) sauce

TIP

The sauce thickens on the pasta as it sets. If you serve as a leftover, drizzle 1 to 2 tablespoons (15 to 28 ml) of water over the pasta and mix in while reheating on the stove top. Use more water as needed to loosen it back up until the pasta is heated through.

FUSS-FREE FRENCH BREAD PIZZAS

Raise your hand if frozen French bread pizzas were your jam when you were a kid. I'm raising both of my hands because of these and pizza rolls. In this vegan version, I use the broiler so the insides of the bread stay fluffy and get warm while the outside gets crispy giving you the perfect bite with a flaky crust and pillowy bread on the inside. I stick with cheese, but add your favorite pizza toppings if you prefer a loaded French bread pizza. Swap out the store-bought vegan shreds with the 3-Minute Cashew Cream Sauce (page 33) drizzled on top if shreds aren't your thing.

+   1 French baguette, cut into a 6-inch (15-cm) long piece, halved (see tip)
+   ¼ cup (60 ml) marinara
+   ¼ cup (59 g) vegan mozzarella shreds
+   1 teaspoon olive oil
+   Toppings of choice (optional)
+   ¼ teaspoon Italian seasoning
+   Crushed red pepper (optional)

Preheat the oven to broil.

Place each side of the baguette with the cutside of the baguette facing up. Divide the marinara between each baguette half and spread generously over the tops. Divide the mozzarella between the baguettes and drizzle ½ teaspoon of olive oil over the mozzarella. Add toppings (if using). Sprinkle Italian seasoning over each half and add crushed red pepper (if using).

Broil for 3 minutes. Rotate the pan and broil for 3 more minutes, until the cheese has melted and the edges have just started to brown. Remove from the oven and let cool to the touch. Serve warm.

Remember all broilers have different intensities. Keep an eye on the bread. If you find that after the first 3 minutes the cheese is melted and the edges have started to brown, there is no need to continue broiling.

YIELD 2 French bread pizzas

TIP

There's no such thing as a baguette that is only 6 inches (15 cm) long. I wanted to clarify before you spend hours at the supermarket losing your mind. Get a French baguette or Italian loaf of bread and slice off 6 inches. How do you determine what 6 inches is? Use a ruler.

PUNK CHEDDAH MAC BAKE

This sauce is a very mild and smooth sauce that's very simple to make because it uses canned pumpkin for the base. This sauce mixed with pasta and topped with a buttery bread crumb topping makes this an irresistible go-to meal to feed the family any night of the week. Don't be afraid to prep this ahead and have it mixed and topped with bread crumbs in advance so you can just pop it in the oven for 30 minutes when you come home from work!

FOR PUNK CHEDDAH SAUCE:

+ 1½ cups (380 g) pumpkin puree
+ ½ cup (68 g) raw cashews, soaked overnight or boiled in water for 10 minutes, drained and rinsed
+ ¼ cup (24 g) nutritional yeast
+ 2 tablespoons (42 g) white miso
+ 3 cups (705 ml) water
+ 1 tablespoon (15 g) Dijon mustard
+ 1 tablespoon (15 ml) soy sauce or gluten-free tamari
+ 1 tablespoon (20 g) maple syrup
+ Juice of ½ lemon
+ 1½ teaspoons sea salt
+ 1½ teaspoons onion powder
+ 1½ teaspoons garlic powder

FOR BAKE:

+ 1 pound (454 g) elbow macaroni pasta
+ Cooking spray
+ 2 tablespoons (28 g) vegan butter, melted
+ ½ cup (25 g) panko or gluten-free panko bread crumbs
+ Paprika (optional)

To make the punk cheddah sauce:
Add the pumpkin, cashews, nutritional yeast, miso, water, Dijon mustard, soy sauce, maple syrup, lemon juice, salt, onion powder, and garlic powder to a blender. Blend for 1 to 2 minutes, until smooth and creamy.

To make the bake:
Preheat the oven to 350°F (175°C, or gas mark 4). Lightly coat a 9 x 13–inch (23 x 33–cm) baking dish or 3-quart baking dish with cooking spray. Prepare the macaroni according to package directions.

Drain the pasta and return it to the pot. Mix in the sauce until all the pasta is coated and transfer it to the prepared baking dish.

Combine the melted butter and panko in a small bowl until the crumbs are coated completely. Sprinkle it over the top of the macaroni and cheese. Sprinkle with paprika (if using).

Bake for 30 to 35 minutes, until the edges of the macaroni and cheese just start to turn golden brown. Serve warm.

YIELD 10 to 12 servings mac bake and 4 cups (940 ml) sauce

TIP

Be extra epic and add an 8-ounce (227 g) bag of vegan cheddar shreds when mixing the sauce and pasta together. It's also worth mentioning that if you prefer fresh pumpkin, by all means, peel, seed, and dice either a butternut squash or sugar pumpkin and cut into cubes. Toss 1½ cups of the cubes in 1 tablespoon (15 ml) of olive oil and roast in an oven at 415°F (213°C, or gas mark 7) for 30 minutes, until browned and fork-tender. Proceed with the sauce recipe as written.

SMOKY KALE AND BLACK BEAN TOSTADA

Smoky kale, crispy tortilla, crunchy fresh veggies, and delicious creamy beans send this delight to the top of my list when feeding any nonvegan. This recipe is inspired by a stop at Green Vegetarian in the San Antonio episode of *The Vegan Roadie*. Top this tostada with Instant Almond Cheese Crumble (page 33) to really blow their minds. If you don't feel like crisping up your tortillas, this recipe can be done as tacos as well. Just fold up your tortillas taco style and fill them up with the goods.

+ 2 tablespoons (30 ml) canola oil or neutral oil of choice, plus more as needed
+ 6 (6-inch/15-cm) corn tortillas
+ ½ onion, roughly chopped
+ 1 red bell pepper, seeds removed and roughly chopped
+ 1 cup (164 g) frozen or fresh corn, thawed if frozen
+ 1 can (15 ounces/425 g) black beans, drained and rinsed
+ 1 teaspoon smoked paprika
+ ½ teaspoon sea salt
+ ½ teaspoon garlic powder
+ ¼ teaspoon black pepper
+ 1 bunch curly kale, stems removed and cut into bite-size pieces

+ Avocado, peeled and cubed
+ Sriracha or hot sauce (optional)
+ Vegan sour cream or 3-Minute Cashew Cream Sauce (page 33, optional)
+ 6 scallions, thinly sliced
+ 6 lime wedges
+ Instant Almond Cheese Crumble (page 33, optional)

Heat 1 tablespoon (15 ml) of canola oil in a large skillet over medium heat. Add the tortillas one at a time, allowing them to crisp up for 40 to 60 seconds on each side and being careful not to let them burn. Transfer to a paper towel–lined plate and repeat until all the tortillas have become crispy and golden brown. Add more oil as needed.

Add the remaining canola oil to the skillet. Add the onion, bell pepper, corn, black beans, smoked paprika, salt, garlic powder, and pepper. Mix until the vegetables and beans are coated with seasoning. Allow the mixture to sit for 3 minutes undisturbed. Mix with a spoon and let sit for 3 minutes, until the corn is cooked throughout and the peppers are soft. Add the kale and continuously stir for 1 minute, until the kale has wilted and evenly distributed.

Divide the mixture atop each tortilla and top with avocado (if using). Drizzle with sriracha, hot sauce, and sour cream (if using). Sprinkle each tostada with scallions, and serve each with a lime wedge to be squeezed over the top. Sprinkle with Instant Almond Cheese Crumble (if using).

YIELD 6 tostadas

TIP

Deglaze the pan with lime juice if you find you have bits of goodies from the veggies and beans stuck to it. Before adding the kale, push the mixture to one side, squeeze ½ a lime on the empty side, and scrape and stir the bits from the pan using the juice to loosen it. Repeat on the other side.

CREAMY SHIITAKE AND CAULIFLOWER RICE RISOTTO

What a gift cauliflower rice has become when I'm trying to watch my calorie intake. It allows me to feel as though I'm having something truly decadent with the calories slashed right in half. This hearty cauliflower risotto gives you all the creamy goodness you want with crisp fresh veggies, and the perfect touch of umami flavor comes through from the sautéed shiitakes. Just be sure to prep your cream sauce and cauliflower rice before you turn on your heat. Even with that prep, this dish comes together easily in 30 minutes flat.

+ ½ cup (120 ml) 3-Minute Cashew Cream Sauce (page 33) or vegan sour cream

+ 2 tablespoons (32 g) white miso paste

+ 2 tablespoons (30 g) Dijon mustard

+ ¾ teaspoon sea salt

+ ½ teaspoon black pepper

+ 2 tablespoons (28 g) vegan butter

+ 1 onion, roughly chopped

+ 5 ounces (140 g) shiitake mushrooms, sliced

+ 1½ cups (225 g) frozen peas

+ 4 cloves garlic, minced

+ 4 cups (960 g) Cauliflower Rice for the Win (page 32)

+ Chopped fresh parsley (optional)

+ Vegan parmesan or Instant Almond Cheese Crumble (page 33, optional)

+ Crushed red pepper (optional)

Add the cashew cream sauce, miso, Dijon mustard, salt, and pepper to a bowl. Whisk until well combined. Set aside.

Heat the butter in a large skillet over medium heat. Add the onion and mushrooms. Sauté for 4 to 6 minutes, until the onions are soft and the mushrooms have reduced in size. Add the peas and sauté for 2 minutes, until heated through. Add the garlic and sauté for 1 minute, until fragrant. Add the cream mixture and stir until everything is coated in the cream.

Add the cauliflower rice and mix until everything is well combined. Allow to cook for 2 minutes, until heated through, but do not overcook or the cauliflower will become soft and mushy. Garnish with parsley, vegan parmesan, and crushed red pepper (if using).

YIELD 4 servings

TIP

This is very versatile. Add any vegetables you love! It's great in the summer with seasonal garden vegetables or in the fall with roasted squash. Just remember to cook the vegetables first and add the cauliflower last to keep the cauliflower from getting soggy or mushy, and you'll be all set!

EASY BAKE BLACK BEAN AND CORN ENCHILADAS

I love enchiladas because they make super tasty leftovers! These come together so easily and offer the perfect flavor and texture combination of creamy beans and crunchy corn with the chilies for just a subtle kick. Make them as they are and then get creative swapping out and adding ingredients that you love.

+ Cooking spray
+ 2 (10 ounces/280 g) cans red enchilada sauce, divided
+ 1 can (15 ounces/425 g) black beans, drained and rinsed
+ 1½ cups (246 g) frozen or fresh corn, thawed if frozen
+ 1 can (4 ounces/115 g) green chilies
+ ½ teaspoon sea salt
+ ½ teaspoon chili powder
+ 10 (6-inch/15-cm) flour or corn tortillas (see tip)
+ ¾ cup (88 g) vegan cheddar shreds or Punk Cheddah sauce (page 157)
+ Vegan sour cream or 3-Minute Cashew Cream (page 33, optional)
+ 6 scallions, thinly sliced

Preheat the oven to 425°F (220°C, or gas mark 7). Lightly grease a 9 x 13-inch (23 x 33–cm) baking dish or pan with cooking spray. Coat the bottom of the baking dish with 1 can of enchilada sauce.

In a bowl, combine the black beans, corn, chilies, salt, and chili powder. Add ¼-cup (60-ml) scoop of the bean mixture to a tortilla, roll up the tortilla, and place it seam-side down in the prepared baking dish. Repeat with remaining tortillas. Pour the remaining can of enchilada sauce over all the enchiladas, and sprinkle with cheddar shreds.

Bake for 30 minutes, until the cheese is melted and the edges of the tortillas have started to brown.

Serve with a drizzle or dollop of sour cream (if using) and a sprinkle of scallions.

YIELD 12 enchiladas

TIP

I prefer flour tortillas when making enchiladas simply because they are more pliable. The 6-inch (15-cm) ones are traditionally labeled "fajita tortillas" in the supermarket. The corn tortillas offer a gluten-free option and are equally delicious. If using corn tortillas, it will be helpful to warm them in the microwave or oven briefly before assembling the enchiladas so they don't crack when rolling them up.

CHAPTER EIGHT

SWEET TREATS: SWEET DREAMS ARE MADE OF THESE!

CINNAMON-SUGAR NICE CRISPY TREATS

We know these treats, and we love these treats! Thank heavens for brands like Dandies Marshmallows, who have been offering up vegan marshmallows since 2009. Fluffy, puffy, sweet, delicious, and all vegan. These treats have just a little extra added touch of cinnamon sugar, always a crowd-pleaser!

+ 1 tablespoon (13 g) organic cane sugar
+ 2 teaspoons (5 g) ground cinnamon, divided
+ Cooking spray
+ ¼ cup (55 g) vegan butter
+ 1 bag (10 ounces/283 g) vegan mini marshmallows
+ 5 cups (750 g) crispy rice cereal

In a small bowl, combine the sugar and 1 teaspoon cinnamon. Set aside.

Spray an 8 x 8–inch (20 x 20–cm) baking dish with cooking spray.

Add the butter and remaining cinnamon to a large saucepan and melt over medium-low heat. Add the marshmallows, stirring constantly, until melted. Remove from the heat and quickly add the cereal to the saucepan. Stir until all pieces are equally coated.

Coat a spatula with cooking spray. Transfer the mixture to prepared baking dish using the prepared spatula (or your hands) and press the mixture into the baking dish until the top is flat and even. Sprinkle generously with cinnamon-sugar mixture.

Let cool completely and cut into 12 squares.

YIELD 12 squares

TIP

Mix in your favorite extras! Add chocolate chips, dried cranberries, dried cherries, pistachios, cocoa powder, or whatever your little heart desires! These treats are a great canvas to customize to your taste or surprise someone on a special occasion by adding one of their favorite ingredients.

GOOEY SNICKERDOODLE OAT BROWNIES

I've always loved snickerdoodle cookies. This is just a little twist on a favorite! This dessert is a fun one to put together with kids. It has the sweet and cinnamony delight of a cookie with the added swirl of butter, sugar, and oat crumble that create gooey cracks in the brownie as it bakes. Try to eat just one.

+ Cooking spray
+ 1 cup (125 g) all purpose or gluten-free all-purpose flour
+ 1½ teaspoons baking powder
+ 1 teaspoon sea salt, divided
+ 2 teaspoons (5 g) cinnamon, divided
+ ¾ cup (150 g) organic cane sugar
+ ½ cup (120 ml unsweetened soy or almond milk
+ 2 tablespoons (30 ml) canola oil
+ 1 teaspoon vanilla
+ 2 tablespoons (28 g) vegan butter, melted
+ ¼ cup (24 g) gluten-free rolled oats
+ ¾ cup (113 g) light brown sugar

Preheat the oven to 350°F (175°C, or gas mark 4). Line an 8 x 8–inch (20 x 20–cm) baking dish with 2 inches (5 cm) of parchment paper with paper overhanging on 2 sides and lightly spray with cooking spray.

In a large bowl, whisk together the flour, baking powder, ½ teaspoon salt, 1 teaspoon cinnamon, sugar, milk, canola oil, and vanilla until smooth. Transfer to the prepared the baking dish.

In a small bowl, combine the butter, rolled oats, brown sugar, remaining salt, and remaining cinnamon. Sprinkle the mixture over the top of the batter.

Bake in the oven for 45 minutes, until the top appears dry. Let cool completely. Pull the entire brownie out of the pan using the overhanging sides of the parchment paper and transfer to a cutting board. Cut into 9 squares.

YIELD 9 squares

TIP

Make a snickerdoodle brownie sundae with this as the base topped with vanilla ice cream, fudge, and caramel sauce! There are recipes for all three in the first *Epic Vegan* book. The bottom of this is stickier than a traditional brownie, making the parchment paper very useful for easy removal from the pan and cutting into squares.

CHERRY LIMEADE COBBLER BARS

Sweet cherries and tart lime with irresistible buttery shortbread crust—and they're in bar form, convenient for a picnic or even a road trip! I love taking these to a summer gathering cut up into squares in a reusable container that doubles as a gift for the host. This way I'm left empty-handed and don't have to worry about forgetting the baking dish! Another plus to this being bars and not a traditional cobbler is that you can eat it with your hands.

+ Cooking spray
+ ½ cup (112 g) vegan butter, melted
+ ½ cup (100 g) organic cane sugar
+ 1½ cups (188 g) all-purpose or gluten-free all-purpose flour
+ ½ teaspoon baking soda
+ ½ teaspoon baking powder
+ ¼ teaspoon sea salt
+ 1 bag (10 to 12 ounces/ 280 to 240 g) frozen cherries, roughly chopped
+ Zest and juice of 1 lime
+ 1 tablespoon (8 g) cornstarch

Preheat the oven to 375°F (190°C, or gas mark 5). Lightly grease an 8 x 8–inch (20 x 20–cm) baking dish with cooking spray.

In a bowl, cream together the butter and sugar (see tip on page 168 to cream without a stand or hand mixer).

Add the flour, baking soda, baking powder, and salt. Mix until well combined. Measure ¾ cup (175 ml) of the mixture from the bowl and set aside. Add the remainder of the mixture to the prepared baking dish and press firmly into the dish into a flat layer. Use the back of a spatula or your fingertips to really press it down into an even flat layer.

In the same bowl, mix in the cherries, lime zest, lime juice, and cornstarch until the cherries are evenly coated. Transfer to a baking dish and spread evenly over the layer of pressed crust.

Sprinkle the remaining crust mixture over the cherries and lightly pat it down so it sticks into the cherry filling. Bake for 45 minutes, until the top is golden. Cool completely before cutting. Putting it in the freezer for an hour will do the trick to rush things along, but I like to let them set overnight. Cut into 16 squares.

YIELD 16 squares

TIP

For a shortcut, chop the cherries by adding them to the food processor and pulsing just a few times. If you don't have a hand zest or microplane, use the smallest grater section of a cheese grater to zest the lime.

PB & J BANANA MUFFINS

Everyone loves peanut butter and jelly! Paired with the perfectly baked goodness of a banana muffin, it's a delight for any age. Peanut butter and jelly isn't just for the kiddos! Depending on the size of your bananas, you may have more or less batter than needed, give or take a muffin or two. If you end up with a tiny bit more batter, divide it by the teaspoon onto the muffins ready to go in the oven!

+ ¼ cup (60 ml) canola oil
+ ½ cup (130 g) creamy peanut butter
+ 1 cup (225 g) packed light brown sugar
+ ½ teaspoon sea salt
+ 1 teaspoon baking soda
+ 2 teaspoons (10 ml) vanilla extract
+ 2 ripe bananas, mashed
+ 1½ cups (188 g) all-purpose or gluten-free all-purpose flour
+ 1 tablespoon (15 g) roasted peanuts, crushed
+ ¼ cup (60 ml) jelly of choice

Preheat the oven to 350°F (175°C, or gas mark 4). Line a 12-cavity muffin pan with cupcake liners.

Combine the canola oil and peanut butter in a bowl, and mix until smooth and creamy. Add the brown sugar and cream together with a spoon, hand mixer, or stand mixer. Add the salt, baking soda, vanilla, and mashed bananas. Mix until well combined. Add the flour and mix until well combined. Do not overmix.

Transfer ¼ cup (60 ml) of the batter to each liner of the prepared pan.

Bake for 15 minutes. Remove from the oven and add 1 teaspoon of jelly to each muffin top using a teaspoon. Create a small indent in the muffin when putting the jelly on top so it sets inside the muffin.

Return to the oven to bake for 18 to 20 minutes, until the top edges of the muffin have browned. Remove from the oven, and sprinkle ¼ teaspoon crushed peanuts over each muffin top. Sprinkle right onto the jelly so it sticks. Let cool completely.

YIELD 12 muffins

TIP

A stand or hand mixer is not necessary to cream sugar and butter. However, if using a spoon, sometimes it helps to press the soft butter into the sugar with the tines of a fork to break it up first and then cream with a spoon until fluffy and smooth. Easy peasy.

NO-CHURN PINEAPPLE BASIL SORBET

Pineapple and basil are a dream combo. Sweet and just a touch earthy with tropical notes. A fun variation on this recipe is to pour this mixture into popsicle molds! The faster you move from blending to freezer, the less icy the final sorbet will be. If you have xanthan gum in your arsenal of ingredients, you can always add ¼ teaspoon to the blender. This will aid maintaining a smooth mouthfeel and overall avoidance of an icy texture, but it's unnecessary. This is perfect for a summer day! If you have a blender that can't quite get this smooth, add 1 tablespoon (15 ml) of pineapple or orange juice as needed to get things moving.

+ 1 bag (16 ounces/455 g) frozen pineapple tidbits
+ 1 can (20 ounces/567 g) crushed pineapple, with juices
+ ½ cup (120 ml) agave
+ ¼ cup (10 g) packed fresh basil

Add the frozen pineapple, crushed pineapple and its juices, agave, and basil to a blender. Blend just long enough to reach a smooth consistency. Do not overblend as the frozen pineapple will begin to warm and the texture of the sorbet will get icier.

Transfer to a standard-size loaf pan, and press plastic wrap to the top of the mixture to push all of the air out of the pan. Freeze overnight.

YIELD 8 servings

TIP
If you wish to use 2 cups (330 g) of fresh pineapple in place of the frozen, you will need to use an ice cream maker. An ice cream maker will aerate the mixture and keep the ice crystals small so the texture does not get too icy.

SO EASY SUNBUTTER COOKIES

It was the summer of 2009 and I mistakenly purchased sunflower butter instead of peanut butter while shopping at the busiest Trader Joe's in the world (you feel me, Union Square NYC Trader Joe's). This was the best mistake I have ever made! I immediately became obsessed with the sweet and salty (and lighter, in my opinion) alternative to peanut butter. I'm so addicted to it, I used it in my traditional peanut butter cookie recipe to make these equally addictive delights! Careful, you can't eat just one.

+ ½ cup (112 g) vegan butter, room temperature
+ ¾ cup (195 g) creamy sunflower butter
+ 2 teaspoons (10 ml) vanilla extract
+ 1 cup (225 g) light brown sugar
+ 1¼ cups (157 g) all-purpose or gluten-free all-purpose flour
+ ¾ teaspoon baking soda
+ ½ teaspoon sea salt
+ Water, as needed

Preheat the oven to 350°F (175°C, or gas mark 4). Line a sheet pan with parchment paper.

In a bowl or stand mixer, cream together the butter, sunflower butter, vanilla, and brown sugar. Add the flour, baking soda, and salt. Mix until a firm dough forms; depending on the sunflower butter you use, the dough may be dry. If it is crumbly, add water 1 tablespoon (15 ml) at a time until it all sticks together. The dough shouldn't be wet.

Form balls made of 2 level tablespoons and place them on the prepared sheet pan at least 2 inches (5 cm) apart. Smash the tops down with a fork creating the traditional peanut butter cookie grid-style design (see tip). Bake for 12 to 14 minutes, or until the edges are just slightly browned.

Let cool completely on the pan.

YIELD 18 cookies

TIP

To create the traditional grid marks seen on peanut butter cookies in bakeries across the world, simply press the back of a fork on the top of each cookie ball, rolling the dough through the prongs. Repeat this motion, perpendicular to the marks you just made to create the grid.

SALTED CHOCOLATE CHIP SKILLET COOKIE

This cookie is a nod to those delicious cookie cakes that were available at shopping malls back in the day. Maybe they still are; I haven't been to a mall in some time. Anyway, while I do love a birthday cookie cake loaded with frosting, I went with the straightforward version here for a quick and easy cookie cake just right for any occasion! If you do want frosting (and feel free to go the extra mile and pipe your favorite frosting all over this), my favorite buttercream recipe is in the first *Epic Vegan* book.

+ Cooking spray
+ 1 cup (225 g) vegan butter, room temperature
+ ¾ cup (113 g) light brown sugar
+ ¾ cup (150 g) organic cane sugar
+ 3 tablespoons (45 ml) unsweetened soy or almond milk
+ 1 tablespoon (15 ml) vanilla extract
+ 2¼ cups (282 g) all-purpose or gluten-free all-purpose flour
+ 1 tablespoon (8 g) cornstarch
+ 1 teaspoon baking soda
+ 1 teaspoon sea salt, divided
+ 1½ cups (262 g) vegan chocolate chips or mini vegan chocolate chips
+ Vegan vanilla ice cream or Beyond the Cinnamon Roll Sheet-Pan Pancakes Glaze (page 42, optional)

Preheat the oven to 350°F (175°C, or gas mark 4). Lightly grease a 10-inch (26-cm) cast-iron skillet or oven-safe skillet with cooking spray.

In a bowl, cream together the butter, brown sugar, and cane sugar (see tip on page 168 to cream without a stand or hand mixer).

Add the milk and vanilla, and mix until well combined. Add the flour, cornstarch, baking soda, and ¾ teaspoon salt. Mix until well combined; do not overmix. Fold in the chocolate chips until evenly dispersed.

Transfer the dough into the prepared skillet and push the dough out to the sides. Sprinkle with the remaining salt. Bake in the oven for 40 to 45 minutes, until the center appears to be dry and the top is lightly brown.

Remove from the oven and cool completely before serving. Slice like a cake to serve, and top each slice with a scoop of store-bought vanilla ice cream or drizzle of glaze (if using).

YIELD 12 slices

TIP

If you don't have a cast-iron skillet, don't fret: You can still achieve the same results following the recipe as written. Use a traditional 8 x 8–inch (20 x 20–cm) baking dish or pie tin in place of the skillet. Are you impatient? Me too! Sometimes I set this on a sheet pan and cool it in the freezer for 30 minutes and then I disregard my "completely cooled" rule and cut into it and serve warm. The inside will be a little gooey this way, but it's "omg delicious." I hate waiting for sh*t to cool.

NO-BAKE EVERYTHING COOKIES

My sister loved peanut butter no-bake cookies when we were kids. I tried them but never had the fondness she did, until now! I switched it up and added everything I liked to these cookies to suit my taste, and you should do the same! It's called an everything cookie for a reason, so when it comes to the dried fruits, seed, and nuts, swap things in and out to include everything you love. These come together so easy! I love to make them when I have a sweet tooth attack—the only tricky part is not eating all the cookie dough before I give it time to set! Use sunflower butter in place of peanut butter if dealing with a peanut allergy.

+ 1 cup (260 g) creamy peanut butter
+ ½ cup (120 ml) agave
+ ½ cup (120 ml) coconut oil, melted
+ 1½ cups (144 g) gluten-free rolled oats
+ ¼ cup (59 g) oat flour
+ ½ cup (73 g) sunflower seeds
+ ½ cup (70 g) pepitas
+ ½ cup (55 g) chopped pecans
+ 1 cup (120 g) dried cranberries
+ 1 cup (175 g) vegan mini chocolate chips

Line a large sheet pan with parchment paper. While the sheet pan should be large, it should also be able to fit in your refrigerator.

In a bowl, combine the peanut butter, agave, and coconut oil. Mix until well combined. Add the oats, oat flour, sunflower seeds, pepitas, pecans, cranberries, and chocolate chips. Mix until well combined.

Create balls of dough using 2 heaping tablespoons of dough for each ball. Add the balls to the prepared sheet pan and flatten each of them into the shape of a cookie. There is no need to create large gaps between cookies. Put as many on a cookie sheet as you can fit just as long as the sides are not sticking together.

Cover with plastic wrap and refrigerate for 1 hour to firm up. Remove the cookies from the sheet pan. Serve immediately or transfer to an airtight container and store in the refrigerator for up to 14 days.

YIELD 24 cookies

TIP

These should be stored in the refrigerator and never left out at room temperature as they will melt easily.

CRUNCHY PB PRETZEL CHIP BITES

I really like little portion-sized sweet treats. It helps me keep track of how many I eat so I can try to stop myself when I feel like I have had too many. For this one, I combined my favorite things: crunchy pretzel, smooth salty peanut butter, and melt-in-your-mouth chocolate chips. This is a super fun hands-on recipe for kids to make too! Pro tip on pretzel crushing: Add them to a blender or food processor and pulse until crumbs form. Or put the pretzels in a zip-seal bag and lightly smash them with a rolling pin or large end of a wine bottle until crumbs are formed.

+ ½ cup (130 g) creamy peanut butter
+ 3 tablespoons (60 g) maple syrup
+ ¼ teaspoon sea salt
+ ½ cup (118 g) crushed pretzels
+ 2 tablespoons (30 g) oat flour
+ 3 tablespoons (33 g) mini vegan chocolate chips

In a bowl, combine the peanut butter, maple syrup, and salt. Mix until smooth and creamy. Add ¼ cup (58 g) of the pretzel crumbs, oat flour, and chocolate chips. Mix until well combined. Scoop out 1 heaping teaspoon at a time and roll into balls. Set aside.

Put the remaining pretzel crumbs on a plate and roll each ball in the mixture until well coated.

Serve cold or at room temperature (I prefer cold). This will keep in an airtight container for up to 1 week in the refrigerator.

YIELD 16 bites

TIP

If you don't have any oat flour, you can make your own oat flour by blending oats in a blender or food processor until a flour forms. Voila!

CELEBRATION COWBOY COOKIE BARS

Cowboy cookie bars: sweet, decadent, chewy, crumbly, and full of little morsels of chocolate, coconut, and pecans in each bite. Confession: I had never had a cowboy cookie or bar until our dear friends Emily and Kevin gifted my husband and me with a box from a local bakery for our birthday (yes, we share the exact same birthday). After one bite, I was suddenly obsessed. To commemorate my new love affair with these bars, I added sprinkles so these bars will add a festive touch to any celebratory occasion, as they were the perfect treat for our birthday.

+ Cooking spray
+ 2 tablespoons (14 g) flax meal
+ ¼ cup (60 ml) water
+ 1 cup (225 g) vegan butter, room temperature
+ ¾ cup (150 g) organic cane sugar
+ ¾ cup (113 g) dark brown sugar
+ 1 tablespoon (15 ml) vanilla extract
+ 1¾ cups (218 g) all-purpose or gluten-free all-purpose flour
+ 1 teaspoon baking soda
+ ½ teaspoon sea salt
+ 1 cup (96 g) gluten-free rolled oats

+ 1½ cups (120 g) sweetened coconut shreds
+ 1 cup (175 g) mini vegan chocolate chips
+ 1 cup (110 g) chopped pecans
+ ¼ cup (45 g) vegan sprinkles

Preheat the oven to 375°F (190°C, or gas mark 5). Lightly spray a 9 x 13–inch (23 x 33–cm) baking pan with cooking spray.

Add the flax and water to a small bowl, and whisk to combine. Set aside to thicken for 5 minutes.

Cream together the butter, sugar, and brown sugar with a hand mixer or stand mixer until smooth and creamy (see tip on page 168 to cream without a stand or hand mixer).

Add the flax mixture and vanilla to the bowl. Mix until well combined. Add the flour, baking soda, salt, oats, coconut, chocolate chips, and pecans. Mix until everything comes together to form a thick dough.

Transfer the dough to the prepared baking pan and press it into the pan with fingertips or back of a spatula until evenly dispersed in the pan. Sprinkle the sprinkles across the top, and gently press them into the top of the dough.

Bake for 35 minutes, or until the edges have browned and the top looks dry. Let cool completely and cut into 12 bars.

YIELD 12 bars

TIP

Sometimes I cut the bars in half to create 24 rectangle bars. There's a lot going on with these, and I find the smaller bars are better for party settings where guests may have several dessert options they want to sample.

STRAIGHTFORWARD STRAWBERRY ICEBOX CAKE

Icebox cakes are fun! This one goes a step further to utilize the latest on the market available in vegan whipped cream offerings. I've included options for the spray whip and whip available in the frozen section in the tub. My preference is always the tub version, but both work great! The spray can create roughly 2 cups of whipped cream, exactly what this recipe calls for. You can also get the same amount from a tub. This recipe makes a smaller cake as this is best when enjoyed within three hours of making it and perfectly serves four people.

+   2 cups (192 g) vegan whipped cream

+   6 vegan rectangle-shaped graham crackers, 2 cut in half

+   1½ cups (220 g) strawberries, hulled and roughly chopped into small pieces

Add ½ cup (48 g) of whipped cream to a standard-size bread loaf pan. Spread into an even layer to create the base. Add the following layers.

Layer 1:
Add 1 graham cracker plus half of a graham cracker to create one layer. The half of the graham cracker may overlap on the whole graham cracker slightly. Spread ¼ cup (24 g) of whip over the graham cracker, top with ½ cup (75 g) of strawberries, and spread an additional ¼ cup (24 g) of whip over the berries.

Layer 2:
Add 1 graham cracker plus half of a graham cracker to create one layer. The half of the graham cracker may overlap on the whole graham cracker slightly. Spread ¼ cup (24 g) of whip over the graham cracker, top with ½ cup (75 g) of strawberries, and spread an additional ¼ cup (24 g) of whip over the berries.

Final Layer:
Add 1 graham cracker plus a half a graham cracker, ½ cup (48 g) of whipped cream, and ½ cup (75 g) of strawberries. Crumble the remaining half graham cracker into tiny bits and sprinkle it over the top of the top.

Cover with plastic wrap and refrigerate for 1 hour. Cut into 4 slices and serve. Best if eaten within 3 hours.

YIELD 4 pieces

TIP
Swap out the strawberries for your berry of choice such as blueberries, raspberries, or blackberries, or combine them all for a Berry Icebox Cake! I like to make this cake before I prepare dinner. By the time dinner has been served and eaten, the cake is the perfect texture as the graham cracker has softened into what resembles a cake.

MR. BENSON'S PUPPY BITES

While I was writing this book, we adopted Mr. Benson, a sweet little mutt that made our family complete. It has always been important for me to know what ingredients my animals are consuming. For these treats I traditionally use fresh pumpkin or butternut squash (see tip), but I call for canned pumpkin in this recipe to keep it as easy as you need it to be. These come together quickly and can be stored in the refrigerator in an airtight container for up to two weeks—but they won't last that long with your pup begging for more every time you open the refrigerator door.

+ ½ cup (48 g) gluten-free rolled oats
+ 2 pinches ground cinnamon
+ ¼ cup (36 g) canned pumpkin
+ ¼ cup (65 g) creamy peanut butter
+ 1 tablespoon (15 g) oat flour

Add the oats and cinnamon to a bowl, and mix until well combined. Add the pumpkin and peanut butter, and mix until a thick dough forms.

Scoop out 1 heaping teaspoon at a time and roll into balls. Repeat until all dough has been turned into little treats. Sprinkle oat flour over all the bites and roll them around on the plate until they are lightly coated in the flour.

YIELD 16 treats

TIP

You can use fresh pumpkin or butternut squash for this. Just steam it and let cool completely. Mash and use as directed.

SPICED HOT CHOCOLATE S'MORES BROWNIES

This brownie is a variation of the cake I created when I competed in the final round of the Food Network's *Girl Scout Cookie Championship* television show. The cake was a six-layer, two-tiered, double barrel cake featuring chili peppers from a surprise ingredient table and the vegan s'mores Girl Scout cookie. This brownie offers up the chocolatey, spicy, marshmallow ooey gooey fun the cake did, only in one simple layer, one pan, and a fraction of the time. Oh, and also without the pressure of doing it on TV in front of a panel of judges and a dozen cameras on you.

+ Cooking spray
+ 1 tablespoon (7 g) flax meal
+ 2 tablespoons (28 ml) water
+ 2 cups (250 g) all-purpose or gluten-free all-purpose flour
+ 1 cup (200 g) organic sugar cane
+ ¾ cup (66 g) unsweetened cocoa powder
+ 1 teaspoon baking soda
+ 1 teaspoon sea salt
+ 1 tablespoon (7 g) plus 1 teaspoon ground cinnamon
+ 1½ teaspoons chili powder
+ ¼ teaspoon cayenne pepper
+ ¾ cup (175 ml) canola oil
+ ¾ cup (177 ml) unsweetened soy or almond milk
+ 1 tablespoon (15 ml) vanilla extract
+ 1½ cups (262 g) mini vegan chocolate chips
+ 2 cups (210 g) mini vegan marshmallows
+ 1 cup (102 g) roughly crumbled vegan graham crackers

Preheat the oven to 350°F (175°C, or gas mark 4). Line a 9 x 13–inch (23 x 33–cm) baking dish with 3 inches (7.5 cm) of parchment paper hanging over each side of the baking dish and coat with cooking spray.

Combine the flax meal and water in a small bowl. Set aside to thicken for 5 minutes.

In a large bowl, whisk together the flour, sugar, cocoa powder, baking soda, salt, cinnamon, chili powder, and cayenne pepper until well combined. Add the canola oil, milk, vanilla, and flax mixture. Mix with a wooden spoon until well combined. Do not overmix. Fold in the chocolate chips, marshmallows, and graham crackers until combined.

Transfer to the prepared baking dish, spreading the batter evenly to fill the dish. Bake for 35 minutes, until the top is dry and the marshmallows have started to puff and brown slightly. Let cool for 10 to 15 minutes, then lift the entire brownie out of the baking pan with the overhanging parchment. Transfer to a flat surface and cut into 12 pieces.

Store in an airtight container or wrap in plastic wrap. Keep at room temperature for 3 days or store in the freezer for up to 3 months.

YIELD 12 brownies

TIP

Take out the cinnamon, chili powder, and cayenne pepper to have a traditional brownie without the spice. Cut into smaller pieces to create "brownie bites."

ACKNOWLEDGMENTS

In a world full of talented chefs, food bloggers, and influencers, writing cookbooks is a tough business. I'm forever grateful to the team at Fair Winds/Quarto for believing in my mission to create fun, engaging, and welcoming content for everyone, vegans and nonvegans. Amanda Waddell, from the jump on this one, you were as excited as I was, thank you. Lydia Rasmussen, thank you for fearlessly jumping in. Marissa Giambrone and Meredith Quinn: reunited and it feels so good! Thank you for collaborating with me to deliver the best book possible. I would be lost without your talents.

Jenna Nelson Patton, I'm so grateful to you not only for being a fierce copy editor but for also being the cheerleader I never knew I needed. Thank you for helping me make this book as epic as possible and for lending a hand in recipe testing as well.

This book was in the midst of heavy recipe testing when COVID-19 hit and grocery store shelves were cleared out, but that didn't stop us from soldiering onward. Lj Steinig, Patty Herflicker, Christine Pearson, Alison Neuman, Carla Slachert, and Jen O'Neill Smith: Thank you for your handwork and dedication when I'm investigating even the tiniest adjustment of ¼ teaspoon salt. Because of your commitment to recipe testing this book was able to stay on schedule.

A heartfelt thank you to Odelaisy Escobar, Jackie Velasco, Carmella Galvan, Linda Hermosillo, and Alethea Lanus. Your honest feedback made this book be the best it can be. I am grateful for the encouragement and enthusiasm you offered me during this project.

Emily and Kevin Graney: I'm so grateful for your support over the years. Thank you for providing me with a sense of "home" during the writing of this book. Your kindness extends further than you know.

An extra special thank you to Laura VanZandt (@bitsizedbeet) and Natalie Slater (@bakeanddestroy). Humans like you make social media a great place to be. Both of you have lifted me up over the miles (and sometimes in person, hooray!) when I needed it most.

Sunshine, thank you for always being so enthusiastic and supportive about everything I cook and all of my endeavors. It means the world to me.

Ashley Madden, from the day we met my life was changed for the better. Friendships like ours come few and far between in life. I cherish you dearly. Thank you for making the recipes come to life in this book with your stunning photography. I'm looking forward to many more projects with you over the years. I can't imagine my culinary world without you in it.

Thank you to everyone who follows @TheVeganRoadie on social media, watches *The Vegan Roadie*, or purchased my previous books. It's because of you that I have been able to continue my mission to help people eat more veggies! I'm eternally grateful for your encouragement and support.

My husband, David Rossetti, you are the most patient, supportive, and giving human. You pull yourself away from your work selflessly as I hem and haw over the best way to finish off a recipe, give it a punchy title, or search for the best adjective to describe yet another cashew cream sauce. This book is as much yours as it is mine. Thank you for being there for me unconditionally time and again. I love you.

com•pas•sion

/kəm'paSHən/

noun

1. sympathetic pity and concern for the sufferings or misfortunes of others.

The world turned upside down while this book was being written, spring and summer of 2020. I was crushed to see how the human race responded in some instances. But I was hopeful and overwhelmed at the human spirit and the compassion that I witnessed being exercised daily. Don't let the darkness of evil overshadow the good. Consider this simple fact: Compassion is ALWAYS quick and easy. For the animals, for the planet, for each other. Be kind to one another and remember, it's nice to be nice.

Keep on cookin',

Dustin

INDEX

ABOUT THE AUTHOR

Dustin Harder is the host and creator of the original series *The Vegan Roadie* and the podcast *Keep On Cookin'*. A graduate of the Natural Gourmet Institute in New York City, he is a vegan chef and cooking instructor and works in culinary development for restaurants and various food brands. Dustin has been seen on the Food Network and appeared in various publications such as *Eating Well*, *VegNews*, *Vegan Lifestyle Magazine*, *Chowhound*, *Vegetarian Times*, and *Paste* magazine. He is the author of *The Simply Vegan Cookbook*, which was featured by *Forbes* as one of the best vegan cookbooks, and *Epic Vegan*, named one of the best vegan books of 2019 by *Eat This, Not That*.

Learn more about Dustin Harder at veganroadie.com and on Facebook, Instagram, and Twitter (@TheVeganRoadie).